John Baptist Purcell

The Vickers and Purcell Controversy

Respectfully Presented to all the Lovers of Truth

John Baptist Purcell

The Vickers and Purcell Controversy
Respectfully Presented to all the Lovers of Truth

ISBN/EAN: 9783744670944

Printed in Europe, USA, Canada, Australia, Japan

Cover: Foto ©Lupo / pixelio.de

More available books at **www.hansebooks.com**

THE

VICKERS AND PURCELL

CONTROVERSY.

RESPECTFULLY PRESENTED TO ALL THE LOVERS OF TRUTH,

BY

JOHN B. PURCELL,

Archbishop of Cincinnati.

PUBLISHED FOR THE BENEFIT OF MOUNT ST. MARY'S SEMINARY OF THE WEST.

BENZIGER BROTHERS,
PRINTERS TO THE HOLY APOSTOLIC SEE.
CINCINNATI AND NEW YORK.
1868.

Entered, according to Act of Congress, in the year 1868, by

BENZIGER BROTHERS,

In the Clerk's Office of the District Court of the United States, for the Southern District of Ohio.

PREFACE.

The Rev. Thomas Vickers having, for reasons which need not be told, failed to carry out his printed programme of evening lectures in Hopkins' Hall, for the continuance whereof I had waited in vain for several weeks, I now publish, according to promise, my edition of the Controversy.

Notwithstanding the many interruptions to which I was subjected in writing my Letters, by absence from home and arduous ministerial duty, I am constrained to say that, in reviewing those Letters, I can not discover any thing that requires retraction, emendation, or excuse for having been incorrectly stated, or incautiously advanced. On the other hand, I have learned to appreciate more fully the utter shipwreck which Mr. Vickers has made of Christian faith—if he ever had such faith; for in a sermon by him published, I know not how long ago, in the Cincinnati Commercial, of which a slip is now before me, I see that he presents "Queries to the Orthodox Churches"—"No personal Deity in the Universe"—"Angels and Devils Antediluvian Monsters"—"Rejection of Miracles"—"Science proves that Man needs no Saving." To these impieties he adds scoffs at the inutility, the absurdity of prayer. We now more clearly understand why, after denying the personality of God, he calls Christ, who teaches the duty and efficacy of prayer, a "Theological fiction," and the Bible, which inculcates the same salutary and consoling truth, "a Crutch." What justice could the Catholic Church, or any of the so-called orthodox denominations expect or receive at the hands of such a man?

After this introduction to the irreligious character of Mr. Vickers, for which we are indebted to himself, and not another, I now call the reader's attention to some of his misstatements of facts: When asked by me who had chosen him to offer the sympathy of the American population of Cincinnati to the St. John's Society, he replies (p. 95*), "Did I not say expressly, in my sermon of October 13th, that I had been chosen by the St. John's Society?" The sermon is under my eyes, and I can not—nor can any one—see in it those words. What we do read, in the opening sentence, is this: "Rev. Thomas Vickers, of the First Congregational Society, began by saying that he had been chosen to express the sympathy," etc. He does *not* say by whom chosen; and it would have been simply absurd to say he had been chosen by the Society itself to present to it the sympathy of the American population!

On pp. 38* and 79,* he is compelled to eat his own words and Mr. Mohr's about the quotation from Aquinas: "I did not pretend to give the exact words;" "Aquinas did not specify the method by which heretics were to be exterminated." On p. 80,* he says he

---

* Rev. Mr. Vickers' pamphlet.

showed me that Molkenbuhr was "an idiot." He had not so much as used the word, much less proved that it was applicable to that writer. After such exhibitions of the utter recklessness of Mr. Vickers' assertions, it were a loss of time to show how he mistakes *Bouvier de Matrimonio;* but I owe it to the readers of this Controversy to say that my position with regard to *Firmilian* is exactly as I have stated. In a matter of criticism, I am freethinker enough to bow to no man's judgment unless supported by arguments that seem to me satisfactory.—"Nullius addictus jurare in verba Magistri." For the learning of the late Archbishop Kenrick I have always entertained the highest respect; but on more than one occasion I have been compelled to differ from him. Archbishop Tizzani, a living writer, and one of the most learned professors of the College of the Sapienza, Rome, goes farther than I have ventured, to declare the letter of Firmilian a forgery. The Greek-pretended original was never produced. "The Latin translation," says the last number of the Dublin Review, "was attributed gratuitously to St. Cyprian. From beginning to end it has the marks of Donatist manufacture about it." The learned and Most Rev. Professor may not have succeeded in his impeachment of all the other documents connected with the Cyprianic argument, but in this I claim the right to say he has succeeded perfectly.

In my Pastoral Letter, any one who takes up the Pope's Encyclical and Syllabus, as republished and translated by Mr. Vickers, and places them in parallel columns with the Pastoral, will see that I have frankly, squarely, honestly avowed my adhesion to Circular and Syllabus; and

I avow further, that neither contains a single proposition but what I can plainly and fearlessly accept as a Cis-montanist, or an Ultramontanist, a Catholic, or an American citizen.

In Mr. Vickers' edition of the Controversy, he has introduced a sermon which he preached on the words of St. Paul: "Always learning." (2 Tim. iii: 7.) The sermon is the persiflage of the inspired apostle by a grinning satyr. St. Paul teaches that all necessary saving truth, religious truth, was brought us from Heaven by Jesus Christ, the "Author and Finisher of our faith." Mr. Vickers denies that Christ has done any such thing. According to him, we must not believe that we have attained all truth in any thing. We must always be unlearning as well as learning. What we know to-day for truth, he evidently supposes we may discover to be falsehood to-morrow. We can not be sure of the demonstrations of any of the propositions or *theorems* of Euclid, any more than of any of the revelations of heaven; and in propounding this theory, he calumniates the Church, and seeks to stultify his dupes by telling them she claims to have arrived at the last results, the *ne plus ultra*, the Ultima Thule of science. It is thus the Church is rewarded for having, from her very first institution, daily advanced the horizon of science. She does not claim to have reached the last results in astronomy, chemistry, natural philosophy, botany, geology, or any other science: all she claims is that God has intrusted to her the deposit of faith; that he has commissioned her to teach it to all nations to the end of time, he himself preserving her from error, and guiding her unto all truth. She claims that the God of revelation is the God of science also; that these two, proceeding from the same divine source, can never be contradictory; and that the pioneers of science, the explorers of nature, the authors of great inventions, must not pretend that their discoveries authorize them to give the lie to God, or to the Bible. In a word, that there is as much truth as wit and ridicule of science, falsely so-called, in the practical joke played on a club of infidel geologists by the Pickwickian Christian who sent them a square post of stone, four or five feet in height, dug up, or pretended to have been—which is the same thing—from a depth of forty or fifty feet, like a bone of a megalotherion, or a mastodon, with an inscription, which he charged them to interpret, but which puzzled them for days. At last a peasant, who was in the Christian's secret, happened into the club-room, and, after listening for awhile to the discussions, remarked to the laughers at Genesis, they must be a pack of dunces for not seeing the interpretation at once. "Well," they replied, "we suppose you are not a dunce; can you explain it?" "I can," said he; "and so can you, if you divide the syllables of the inscription aright. Do you not see it is 'Forassestorubon'" (For asses to rub on).

In concluding this preface, we would intimate to Rev. Mr. Vickers, that as they are the same sun and moon that enlightened the earth on the day of creation—and they are nothing the worse for age—that enlighten it now, so they are the same truths, revealed by Jesus Christ at the origin of Christianity, that enlighten our religious firmament to-day, and that they, like God, are not affected by years. We would not change for new ones. Let any unbeliever make a new sun and moon before pretending to make for the world a new religion.

Finally, let Mr. Vickers tell us who the Catholics are who are not allowed to read the Bible, or we shall think he stated what was false—which would be unpleasant.

J. B. PURCELL,
Archbishop of Cincinnati.

CONTENTS.

		PAGE.
1.	Sermon of Rev. Thomas Vickers, at the Laying of the Corner-Stone of St. John's Church...............	11
2.	Sermon of Archbishop Purcell at the Blessing of the Corner-Stone of St. Rose's Church................	18
3.	Sermon of Rev. Mr. Vickers in reply to Archbishop Purcell..	24
4.	Reply of Archbishop Purcell to Rev. Mr. Vickers..	40
5.	Reply of Rev. Mr. Vickers to Archbishop Purcell..	50
6.	Archbishop Purcell's Reply to Rev. Mr. Vickers...	62
7.	Letter of Rev. Mr. Vickers to Archbishop Purcell...	80
8.	Letter of Archbishop Purcell to Rev. Mr. Vickers...	91
9.	Reply of Rev. Mr. Vickers..	102
10.	Second Letter of Archbishop Purcell to Rev. Mr. Vickers..	115
11.	Rev. Mr. Vickers' Reply..	127
12.	The Archbishop's Reply to the foregoing..	150
13.	Rogues' Gallery..	163
14.	Review of Rev. Mr. Vickers' First Lecture at Hopkins' Hall. Subject:—"Arnold of Brescia".............	164
15.	Review of Rev. Mr. Vickers' Second Lecture at Hopkins' Hall. Subject:—"Wycliffe".....................	170
16.	Review of Rev. Mr. Vickers' Third Lecture at Hopkins' Hall. Subject:—"John Huss".....................	174
17.	Rev. Thomas Vickers..	184
18.	Review of Rev. Mr. Vickers' Fourth Lecture at Hopkins' Hall. Subject:—"Guttenberg," Savonarola.......	186
19.	Review of Mr. Vickers' Sermons...	194
20.	Dix on the Catholic Church...	198

THE VICKERS AND PURCELL CONTROVERSY.

SERMON OF REV. THOMAS VICKERS,

AT THE LAYING OF THE CORNER-STONE OF ST. JOHN'S GERMAN PROTESTANT CHURCH OF CINCINNATI.

(Published in the Cincinnati *Commercial*, September 30, 1867.)

Rev. Thomas Vickers, of the First Congregational Society, began by saying that he had been chosen to express the sympathy of the American population of our city with the occasion. He had been announced to make a speech in the English language, but he saw such a sea of German faces around him that he could not refrain from addressing the assembly in the German language. Nothing separated men from each other so much as a difference of language. Mountains, rivers, deserts, or seas, were not so great a barrier between the nations, as a difference in the mother tongue. He therefore begged leave, although not a German, or of German origin, to make his speech in the German language. The following is a translation of his remarks:

"Dear Friends: This is a solemn and inspiring occasion. We are met together for the purpose of celebrating one of the most solemn acts of worship in which the modern world can participate—in order, in the name of God and humanity, for the spiritual advantage and improvement of the community in which we live, as a representation and illustration of the indissoluble union between the temporal and the eternal, between heaven and earth, between the deity and humanity, to lay the foundation-stone of a new temple of religion. Yes, it is indeed an inspiring thought, that in the midst of the hurry and impatience of the modern world, in the midst of the noise and press of business, the conflict of material interests, in spite of the pleasure-seeking and superficial spirit of the age, in spite of a soulless and heartless materialism, such acts of worship are still possible, such temples can still be built; in short, that there are still men who have a heart and sense for religion, for whom there is still something higher and nobler than their daily bread and their daily pleasure; something which is more lasting and more consolatory than all the riches and all the honor in the world.

"There are, indeed, others, who have not been swallowed up in the maelstrom of modern life, who take an interest in purely spiritual things: and they also build temples, temples of art and science, but temples of religion they despise. For them, religion is a thing of the past, a legend of times long gone by, no longer a living truth. It is sad that there are people enough of this sort, and will be for a long time to come. But they exist, to the shame and disgrace of the Church. They are a living witness to the hollowness and degradation of ecclesiastical Christianity, to the contradiction, now patent to every man of sense, between the old fables of the middle ages and the grand spiritual acquisitions of the modern world.

"Let us not quarrel with those who have turned away with disgust from the silliness and stupidity of the Church, with fright and horror from her spiritual emptiness. Let us rather seek to abate the evil—to improve our own spiritual status.

"Almost all the nations of antiquity regarded the holy places, the temples which were consecrated to the service of the gods, as at the same time places of refuge, to which the oppressed could flee and feel themselves secure from the persecution of their enemies. Had a slave run away from the ill-treatment of his master, did a conquered warrior wish to escape the vengeance of his enemy, or one accused before the courts wish to flee the threatened penalty of the law—the door of the temple was always open, and he who succeeded in reaching this was, from that moment, under the especial protection of the deity. He whose boldness and impudence led him to pursue his victim thus far, to do him any injury whatever in this sacred place, or to tear him away from its protection, was guilty of the highest, the most abominable crime against God and man.

"This custom, which was of heathen origin, was afterward transferred to Christianity. Under the reign of Constantine the Great, the Christian churches were already regarded as places of refuge for all who desired protection, and in the year 431, and Theodosius II, this privilege was extended to all the courts, passages, gardens, and houses belonging to the domain of the several churches. In the following centuries, the ecclesiastical councils extended this right of the Church still further.

Of course this privilege led to great abuses, not only among the heathen, but also among the Christians; therefore came gradually into disuse, and was finally formally abrogated.

"But this custom had, nevertheless, a profound and noble meaning; there was a true thought at the bottom of this rather rude manifestation. Somewhere on earth a place was necessary where, in the hour of his utmost need, man could feel himself secure from the violence of his fellow-men. Neither in the antique States nor in the middle ages could the State, as such, afford this protection. This was possible only to God, or, in other words, to the Church. But in this, as in so many other things, modern civilization brought changes. The State was obliged to assert its prerogative in opposition to the Church; civil law developed itself; it assumed, as a matter of course, the protection of men against mere physical violence; and thus the ecclesiastical right of refuge, in its traditional form, disappeared.

"But it is not the mission of progressive knowledge to destroy the spiritual essence of supernatural forms, but rather to preserve it. And, my friends, the time seems to have come when we ought to inquire whether, for the modern world, this old ecclesiastical privilege has lost all meaning and significance. Is there no noble sense in which the Church of to-day can be an asylum, a place of refuge. I answer confidently, there is a sense in which the Church not only *can* but *must* be such a place of refuge, if she will not dig her own grave and vanish from the earth; the Church ought to be, and must be, a place of refuge for free thought—a place of refuge, a home for the spirit. Hitherto she has never been this. Every thing else has been protected except free thought. Every thing else has found a refuge in the Church, except free thought. Free thought is the only thing which the Church has never tolerated. Thought she has never tolerated at all, for thought is, in its essence, free, and can not be enslaved; where slavery is, there free thought is not, and can not be.

"There was, indeed, a time in which the Church was the home of all culture and all knowledge, in which the old heroes of science and philosophy, when the night of barbarism fell upon them, took refuge in the monasteries, in the cells of the monks. But how was it possible that they could feel themselves at home in such company? As one, in crossing the Alps, gladly takes refuge in the friendly *hospice* while the storm rages without, and does not scorn to pass an hour in conversation with its well-fed monks, who, however, seldom betray any appreciation of that which lies beyond their limited circle of vision, and consequently makes it easy to part from them, so those old spiritual heroes of Greek and Roman antiquity spent the night of the 'Dark Ages' with the monks of the Catholic Church, chatted with them now and then, but wisely kept their own counsel in regard to all problems of a more profound nature, and with the first dawn of the new morning, joyfully went their way toward a more congenial companionship. To drop the metaphor, the Church was for centuries almost the only representative of science and culture, but the world has, after all, little to thank her for, except the preservation and transmission of the spiritual treasures of antiquity. It was never possible for the mind to develop itself under her dominion;

wherever free thought attempted to show itself it was immediately crushed out. There was plenty of dead erudition, but living investigation and freethinking— none at all. It is true, that, as the new era began to dawn, the Church founded numerous universities, but not for the purpose of free mental development, such as we now demand, but for the purpose of training spiritual prize-fighters, whose mission was to defend the dogmas of the Church and to increase the authority of the clergy. Just as soon as such a one began to think for himself she led him to the stake.

"So it has been, my friends, and so it has remained, down to the present hour. The Church, as such, whether she be Roman Catholic or Protestant, has undergone no essential change in this respect. To her, free thought and free investigation are just as heretical as ever they were. But free thought has taken bloody vengeance upon her. To-day she is forsaken of all thinkers; she is the object of mockery and contempt. She has banished free thought from her hearth-stone, and while it goes on conquering and to conquer, subjecting the whole world to its rule, she herself has become a prey to the rats and mice of history. Well for her, if even in this, 'the eleventh hour,' she repent and mend her ways. She must become the asylum, the home of free thought. It is only in the distant future, if at all, that she can become again, and in reality, the representative of all knowledge and culture. For the present her mission is to become *the mirror* of the scientific knowledge of our time; she must appropriate to herself whatever facts of science, history, and criticism the modern age has to offer her. She must digest them, and reproduce them unalloyed. She must 'stoop to conquer;' she must learn of the world in order to win it for herself.

"And, finally, my friends, as it is the mission of every living ecclesiastical community to reconcile modern science and modern consciousness to religion, to mediate between Church and civilization, so, as a German church, on American soil, it is your especial mission, so far as it lies in your power, to procure for German civilization—and by that I mean German scientific culture and German depth of thought and feeling—its proper acknowledgment and its rightful influence in this your adopted home. And to this end I, as the only representative on this platform of the Anglo-American part of our population, offer you my hand and heart. Let us, then, in the expectation of a new era of spiritual freedom, and with the resolution to work for it, lay the corner-stone of this new temple of the religion of the spirit, and may the blessing of God rest upon it."

SERMON OF ARCHBISHOP PURCELL,

AT THE BLESSING OF THE CORNER-STONE OF ST. ROSE'S CHURCH.

(Published in the *Catholic Telegraph*, October 9, 1867.)

[The corner-stone of St. Rose's German Catholic Church, of this city, was blessed by Archbishop Purcell, on Sunday, October 6, 1867, on which occasion he delivered the following sermon:]

BELOVED BRETHREN: At the close of the interesting ceremonies which you have just witnessed, permit me to direct your attention for a few moments to the utterances of a Congregational minister, at the laying of the corner-stone of the St. John's German Protestant Church, in this city, on the 29th of September.

The reverend gentleman to whom I allude, is reported in one of our city papers, of the 30th ult., to have, as it seems to me, and as I think it will to you, involved himself in palpable contradictions, to have stated as truisms what I can not help regarding as glaring misstatements; and to have wantonly and gratuitously insulted the church organization to which he volunteered to speak the sympathy of our American population.

The contradiction is this: In one place he tells us there was indeed a time in which the Church was the home of all culture and all knowledge, in which the old heroes of science and philosophy, when the night of barbarism fell upon them, took refuge. Now, without stopping to inquire of the gentleman who these old heroes were, whence they had come, and when or by whom they had been educated—questions which we well know he would be puzzled to answer—I shall only ask him how this all culture and all knowledge existed in the Church where he falsely asserts free thought was never tolerated? Thought is essentially free. God made it free, and no tyrant, no power can chain it, neither the power of God, who wills it free, nor the power of man, who can not deprive it of its freedom. How, then, could the Church enslave it, or how could she have been the home of all culture and all knowledge if she had enslaved it? Then, *de jure et de facto*, the statement of Rev. Mr. Vickers is false, and in making it he involves himself in a palpable contradiction. The Church, he says again, was for centuries almost the only representative of science and culture, and in the same breath he pretends to say that she crushed free thought wherever it appeared. Now, was there no free thought illustrated, none exercised by the admirable apologists of Christianity, Tertullian, Justin Martyr, Lactantius, Augustin, Chrysostom, Cyprian, Thomas Aquinas, Copernicus, Christopher Columbus, compared to whom it is no disparagement to Mr. Vickers to say he is a mental pigmy. Were not the martyrs of religion at the same time martyrs of free thought when they nobly dared to speak the truth before the tribunals of paganism, the fasces of the consuls, the roaring of the wild beasts, and the crackling of flames in the amphitheaters? And all these were the obedient children of a Church which put an extinguisher on freedom of thought! *Credat*—M. Vickers. When men chose to use their freedom to err she did not, and she could not hinder them. Arius, Macedonius, Pelagius, Manes, Origen, Luther, Calvin, Zuinglius, Beza, and all the heresiarchs, who fell like withered branches from the tree of life during the long lapse of ages, were not led by her to the stake, any more than Servetus, or the New England witches were, nor did she gather them for an *Auto da fé.*

The world, he says, has little to thank the Church for but the preservation and transmission of the spiritual treasures of antiquity. Well, we incline to think this was a great deal. But will the gentleman deign to inform us who it was that fought the great battle with paganism, Mohammedanism, and barbarism, and won it? Was it not the Church? And for this have we not to thank her? Will he tell us of a single nation on the face of the globe that was converted from idolatry to Jesus Christ except by a missionary of the Catholic Church? And if this is so, have we not something else—have we not a great deal to thank her for—beside the preservation and transmission of the spiritual treasures of antiquity?

The Church, says her reverend reviler, founded numerous universities, but not for the purpose of free mental development, such as we now demand, but for the training of spiritual prize-fighters, whose mission was to defend the dogmas of the Church, etc. Well, for what mission or purpose did Christ found the college of the apostles and send them forth when well trained by him; was it not to be spiritual prize-fighters? Was it not to tolerate no pagan vice or error? Was it not to beat down every height and might that exalteth itself against the knowledge of God, and to bring every understanding—pagan freethinkers who were free from thinking aright—to the obedience of Christ? (2 Cor. x: 5.) Did not Jesus Christ say, that whoever refused to hear the Church should be reputed as a heathen and a publican? (Matt. xviii: 17.) Does he not charge his apostles not to teach more, or less, or otherwise than he had commanded them? (Matt. xxiii: 20.) With these, and sundry other similar texts, staring him in the face, will Mr. Vickers have the hardihood to arraign Jesus Christ of intolerance for interdicting free thought? It is God's truth and not man's thinking that makes men truly free. Did not St. Paul interdict freedom of thought and freedom of speech in those against whom he charged his disciple Timothy for having gone astray and turned to vain talking, desiring to be teachers of the law, not understanding what they say, or whereof they affirm? (1 Tim. i: 6, 7.) Did St. Paul stand up for the freethinking of those who, when they knew God, did not glorify him as such, but became foolish in their thoughts, and their senseless hearts were darkened; for saying they were wise, they became fools. (Rom. i: 21, 22.) The Catholic universities, then, would have been repudiated by Jesus Christ, if instead of keeping and guarding faithfully "the form of sound words," they had, under pretext of allowing freethinking, permitted Gospel truths to be denied, and the name of Christ blasphemed, and his holy religion itself obliterated from a world which he had brought it from heaven to redeem. No, Christians, the Church leaves to the human mind all needful liberty. She refuses it none but what is "a cloak for malice."

She gives it a charter like that of the ocean, to roll its mountain billows as it listeth, but she sets it at the same time a barrier from which its proud swelling waves must retire. The Church, says Mr. Vickers, whether she be Catholic or Protestant—take heed to this compliment, reverend pastors and people of St. John's and other Protestant organizations of Cincinnati—the Church, whether Catholic or Protestant—Mr. Vickers is happily of neither, he is a freethinking Congregationalist—has undergone no essential change in this respect. To her free thought and free investigation are just as heretical as ever they were. And for this she has become a prey to the rats and mice of history. Whether this be true or not of Protestantism, Mr. Vickers may be the best judge; but even if he were one of the noxious little animals, he should know by this time, at least, that though they may gnaw a parchment, the foundations of the Catholic Church are too deep, her walls too massive, her battlements too divinely guarded to be in the slightest danger from such sappers and miners. But as for us Catholics, who are the children of the saints, and who look for that life which God will give to those who never change their faith from him, we place, adjust, and bless this corner-stone, not for a tower of Babel, for which the speech we have reviewed might be appropriate, but for a Christian temple. We place, adjust, and bless it, not for freethinking, free-talking, free-loving, free any thing, but in the name of the Father, and the Son, and the Holy Ghost, that true faith may flourish here with the wholesome fear of God and brotherly love; that it may be a house of prayer, that the name of the Lord Jesus Christ may be invoked and praised, and his holy sacraments administered in it; in a word, that a mystic ladder—such as the patriarch beheld in his dream in the wilderness—may be established here, on which the angels of God may descend and ascend, bringing down his blessings from heaven to earth, and taking back the homage of loving, believing grateful hearts to him, the Father of lights, from whom every good and perfect gift, with true religion, comes down to men.

A SERMON BY REV. THOMAS VICKERS,

IN REPLY TO ARCHBISHOP PURCELL.

(Published in the Cincinnati *Gazette*, October 14, 1867.)

TEXT.—And they worshiped the beast, saying, Who is like unto the beast? who is able to make war with him?—REV. xiii: 4.

DEAR FRIENDS: I ought, perhaps, by way of introduction to what I have to say to you this morning, to state briefly the occasion of my sermon. It is known to you that I was invited by the St. John's German Protestant Society, of this city, to participate in the ceremony of laying the corner-stone of their new church edifice. I felt bound by the importance of the occasion, by the fact that the St. John's Society stands committed to liberal Christianity, and by my own position as minister of the only church in our city which acknowledges no bonds of sect or creed, to utter my deepest convictions in regard to the mission of the living Church to the present age. In attempting to impress upon the minds of my hearers the precise nature of this mission, I could not very well help referring to the history of the Church in general, and to its present condition; and referring to it with this distinct object in view, I could not choose but run the risk of giving offense in various directions. Not that I wished to offend any body—far from it; but you can never "tell the truth and shame the devil," without the devil rising up against you and seeking to devour you. So it was in this case. I was obliged, by the truth of history, to say that the Church had hitherto tolerated every thing but thought—this she had never tolerated; that she had been a sanctuary for every thing else, but wherever free thought had attempted to show itself, she had trampled it under foot. I asserted this of the Church in general, as an organized institution, making no exception in favor of any ecclesiastical body. It seems, however, that I committed a very grave offense in not excepting the Roman Catholic Church from these charges. For this offense, Archbishop Purcell undertook, last Sunday, on the occasion of laying the corner-stone of St. Rose Church, to inflict upon me the only ecclesiastical punishment which, in our country, God be thanked, he or any other priest is permitted to administer—he preached a sermon against me. It is this sermon to which I intend to offer some reply to-day.

I am bound to say, at the outset, that I have no personal quarrel with Archbishop Purcell, no personal grievance to redress; that were there no supreme issue at stake, no dangerous falsehood to unmask, no truth to defend, no point to be made in favor of the modern age and its spiritual needs as against the arrogance and despotism of a rotten ecclesiastical institution, I should gladly let all such archiepiscopal expectorations go unnoticed to that early oblivion to which the common sense of the age consigns them. I furthermore hold myself excused from replying to intellectual rowdyism in its own dialect. I leave such fine terms as "mental pigmy," and "reverend reviler," and all such theological shillalahs, to those who, by education and breeding (or the want of these), are accustomed to their use.

Now, that you understand the issue, let us proceed to the matter in hand. Let us see whether I involved myself in "palpable contradictions;" whether I made charges in one breath which I virtually took back in the next. I admitted, on the one hand, that there had been a period in which the Church was the home of all culture and all knowledge, but asserted on the other, that free thought had never been tolerated within her borders—this is the alleged palpable contradiction. And there is, indeed, a contradiction here, but a very different one from that which the Archbishop meant to satirize—one which is the most biting satire upon the whole Roman Catholic institution. It does not require a very large measure of scholastic acumen to distinguish between a contradiction *in the statement of facts*, and a contradiction *in the facts themselves;* the one is a logical blunder, the other an historical one; the one is generally the cause of merriment at the stupidity of him who makes it, the other is the cause of great historical convulsions, the ruin of States, the downfall of dynasties, and the destruction of peoples. Take an example: it was the latter kind of contradiction—the contradiction between a republican form of government and the institution of slavery—which involved this country in a terrific war of four years' duration. It is the same contradiction, the conflict between republicanism and slavery, which has just resulted in our own State in the momentary triumph of despotism, the refusal on no ground of intelligence, but simply on the ground of a difference in the color of the skin, to confer the rights of citizenship on a whole race of men who nobly bear its burdens. That is the kind of contradiction which, if not removed, will yet break this nation to atoms. And this is the kind of contradiction which my address, at the laying of the corner-stone of St. John's Church, intended to illustrate—the contradiction was in the facts, and not in the statement.

It is an old trick of the sophists to distract the attention of their hearers from the chief points at issue, by simply mentioning them, and then passing them by as of no consequence to the argument, while they devote all their forces either to the creation of false issues or to the refutation of that which is merely incidental. It is a fine sample of this sophistry when the Archbishop says he will not stop to inquire "who those old heroes of science and philosophy were," who, when the night of barbarism fell upon them, took refuge in the monasteries of the Catholic Church; he will not stop to inquire "whence they had come, when or by whom they had been educated," for he assumes to know that these are questions which I should be "puzzled to answer." But this happens to be one of the points about which I must compel him to stop and inquire. The heroes to whom I referred were the poets, historians, and philosophers of ancient Greece and Rome. Is it any great task for a scholar to answer the question where these came from, when and by whom they were educated? Or did the Archbishop mean it to be understood that the Roman Church educated them, men who lived centuries, some of them almost millenniums, before she came into existence? To be sure, it would require no extraordinary display of archiepiscopal dialectics to maintain such a thesis, for the new dogma of the "immaculate conception" makes Jesus the cause of his own grandmother's having brought his mother into the world without due process of nature.

But let us lay aside the metaphor entirely, and see what the plain facts of the case are. After the fall of the Roman Empire in the West, there was an almost universal loss of that learning which the Greeks and Romans had accumulated. For centuries taste and knowledge had been declining, but the eruption of the barbarian nations had put an end to them entirely. Up to this time there had been some show of learning and culture among the so-called Fathers of the Church, but even that died out. Outside the ecclesiastical order ignorance reigned supreme, but the knowledge found within it was scarcely worthy of the name. I repeat, there was a time when the Church was the home of all culture and all knowledge, but after all, this lamp of learning in the Church shed such a feeble and ineffectual light that it was scarcely distinguishable from the surrounding darkness. It was in the period known as the Dark Ages. The literary treasures of ancient Greece were stowed away in the monasteries, but the language in which they were written was almost entirely forgotten; not one in a hundred of so-called scholars could read them. Even the Latin, the official language of the Church, became so corrupt and barbarous that it could scarcely be called Latin any longer. Now and then there was one who read and copied an old author, or made extracts from the "Fathers" on points of Church doctrine, but thought, as such, was utterly out of the question. There was no inducement to think, the truth had been attained, and he who presumed to question it was worse than a heathen.

Archbishop Purcell asks, with an air of triumph, which no doubt had an immense effect on his peculiar audience, if there was "no free thought illustrated, none exercised by the admirable apologists of Christianity, Tertullian, Justin Martyr, Lactantius, Augustin, Chrysostom, Cyprian, Thomas Aquinas, Copernicus, Christopher Columbus, compared with whom it is no disparagement to Mr. Vickers to say he is a 'mental pigmy?'" I should like, in passing, to recall to the Archbishop's memory an old Latin proverb, which it would be well for him and his church to consider: *Pigmei gigantum humeris impositi plusquam ipsi gigantes vident* (Pigmies standing on the shoulders of giants see further than the giants themselves). Now, in the first place, it is somewhat remarkable that he does not mention a single thinker who lived between the middle of the fifth century and the beginning of the thirteenth, so that there is a period of nearly eight centuries which seems to be pretty "dark" for him also. If the Archbishop had wanted to illustrate the ecclesiastical learning of this period, he could not have done it better than by referring to productions of a somewhat later date— the times were somewhat changed, but then, you know, *the* Church never changes. It would have been much to the point had he named those profound thinkers, those immaculate logicians and poets, Scherschleiferius, Dollenkopfins, Eitelnarrabianus, Mistladerins, and company, who unfolded their heavenly wisdom (a little mixed up, it is true, with earthly sensuality and debauchery) in the *Epistolæ Obscurorum Virorum*.

Columbus and Copernicus are the only ones he mentions who belong to the modern world, and I have yet to learn that these are counted among the "apologists of Christianity." It was certainly a slip of the tongue which allowed these two names to pass the lips of the Archbishop; he probably meant to say Torquemada and Loyola, who, although not strictly apologists of Christianity, are much better examples of his kind of free thought than Columbus and Copernicus.

But to what extent were the other representatives of free thought? Time will not permit me to characterize them all; but we will take a few examples. First of all, Tertullian, a fine specimen of a freethinker. In his book against the heretics he bellows forth: "Admit that they are not enemies of the truth, what have we to do with men who confess that they are still investigating. Since they are still seeking, they are not in possession of any thing; and as they do not possess any thing, they do not believe, are not Christians. *Nobis curiositate opus non est post Christum, nec inquisitione post evangelium. Cum credimus, nihil desideramus ultra credere.* (After Christ we have no need to desire to know any thing further, after the Gospel no need of inquiry. Since we believe, we desire nothing beyond belief.) What have Athens and Jerusalem, what the Academy and the Church, in common?" This same Tertullian was one of the most blatant, foul-mouthed, and narrow-minded of all the so-called Fathers—the man who took a swinish pleasure in defiling the most sacred names of antiquity, as the Romish Church has always defiled those who disagreed with her. It is furthermore not unessential to mention, before leaving him, that he belonged to a sect which was regarded as heretical and excommunicated by the main body of Christians, and that he never recognized the supremacy of the Roman Bishop.

This brings me to Cyprian, Bishop of Carthage, who, however little of a freethinker he was, was far too free in one respect for Rome. He was the great champion of the unlimited power of each bishop in his own diocese, but a bitter opponent of Roman supremacy; he recognized no *episcopus episcoporum*, and so Bishop Stephen, of Rome, cut off all intercourse with him, and he died in virtual excommunication.

And now for St. Augustin: I take it for granted that whenever a man is capable of free thought and impartial investigation, he is not only willing to accord it to others, but desirous of doing so. And yet it is to this man above all others to whom the Romish Church looks for her authority to punish heretics. Embittered by his controversies with the Danatists, he was the first man in the occident to elaborate a theory for compulsion in religious matters for the persecution of heretics. All later defenders of the right of the Church to use violence do little more than repeat his arguments. And Thomas Aquinas is one of these. You would search in vain for the least vestige of independent thought in the whole three and twenty folios of his writings. His mission was to reduce the dogmas of the Church to the forms of the Aristotelian philosophy, so far as the philosophy was then understood. For the development of free thought there was not an inch of space. The outlines of the picture were all there; it was his office so to put on the Aristotelic colors. But just as little liberty of thought as he himself enjoyed, just so much, and no more, he was willing to tolerate in others. "Heretics," said the Church, "are the sons of Satan, and, therefore, it is nothing but right that, even in this life, they should participate in the lot of their father—*burn, as he does.*" And Thomas Aquinas, in his *Summa Theologiæ*, the great text-book of Roman Catholic theology even at the present day, opposes to all biblical reasons for toleration or milder treatment the words of the apostle, that a heretic should be rejected after the second admonition, to which words he adds the commentary, that *the best way of rejecting him is to execute him;* and, furthermore, that, in the case of apostates, not even an admonition is necessary—these *ought to be burned without further ceremony.* (Summa i, 2, q. 11, art. 3–4.) Are not these men—with whose high-sounding names the Archbishop filled his mouth so full—are they not grand representatives of free thought?

But let us return, for a moment, to Columbus and Copernicus, and ask what the "Holy Catholic Church" was doing while they were making their immortal discoveries in heaven and earth. Their lives cover a period of nearly a century, from about the middle of the fifteenth to the middle of the sixteenth. What a grand age it was; the age in which Bartholomæus Diaz, Vasco de Gama, the Cabots, Vespucci, and Magellan discovered the earth; the age when the fugitive Greeks brought the knowledge of the classics to Italy; when the Humanists, Reuchlin, Erasmus, Hutten, and their compeers, began to combat the ignorance and stupidity of the monks, and Guttenberg lent them his powerful aid; the age in which Raphael, Leonardo da Vinci, Correggio, Michael Angelo, achieved their glorious works; the age of Luther and Melancthon, Zwingli and Calvin; in which they dealt such sturdy blows at an equally powerful and unscrupulous hierarchy. What was it with which the Romish Church was chiefly occupied as the sun was painting the dawn of this new day of history with such magnificent colors? Oh, she was trying her best to conjure back the night! She always loved darkness better than light. She was busy persecuting the Jews in Spain, whom she had forced to abjure their ancient faith, but still suspected of a secret allegiance to it. In a little over thirty years, ending with the year 1517, she had burned twelve thousand two hundred persons alive, and punished nearly two hundred thousand others in various ways, either by torture, imprisonment, loss of property, or all put together. She was issuing bulls against witchcraft, and sending her mercenaries into Germany to burn men, women, and children by thousands. She was selling indulgences to get money to build St. Peter's with—licenses to commit any sin whatever, and forgiveness for any that might have been committed—and all for money. She was burning Savonarola for his plain speech against her wickedness, as she had already burned John Huss and Jerome of Prague. She was attempting to annihilate the Hussites, as she had already massacred the Albigenses. She was founding the order of the Jesuits and perfecting its organization—an order in which, in the service of the Church, men are reduced to machines; in which "obedience takes the place of every motive or affection that usually awakens men to activity; obedience, absolute and unconditional, without thought or question as to its object."

Look for a moment at the Inquisition, which at this time was in its glory. What was its object, and what its method of procedure?

Its object was the suppression of heresy in every form. It was an outgrowth of the theory that the Pope is lord over both the souls and the bodies of men. Every-where, where the Inquisition began its work, Papal law was proclaimed, according to which every one was bound, under pain of excommunication, to reveal, within a definite period, every thing he knew of heretics or heretical actions. This obligation was universal and unlimited; no human tie, neither marriage nor blood relationship, nor the duty of gratitude, afforded relief. Sons and daughters were bound, in conscience, to denounce their own fathers and mothers, even if it were probable or certain that the rack and the stake would be their fate. He who failed to confess what he knew of others was treated as a heretic himself; on the other hand, indulgences were granted to all who contributed to the seizure and punishment of heretics. He who acknowledged himself guilty, and recanted, suffered severe and ignominious punishment, often imprisonment for life; he who remained firm to his convictions was delivered over to the secular arm, with the mocking recommendation: *ut quam clementissime et citra sanguinis effusionem puniretur* (that the punishment be as merciful as possible, and without effusion of blood). This was the atrocious formula for burning alive. The civil power had no choice; under pain of excommunication, the ecclesiastical verdict must be immediately carried into effect, and the victim burnt. Concerning the guilt or innocence of the condemned, the secular courts had nothing to say: their only office was that of the executioner. Even as late as the seventeenth century, one of the most distinguished doctors of canon law, Pignatelli, maintained that even if the secular authorities knew, with certainty, that a sentence was unjust, or rendered void by some flaw in the procedure, they must execute it, nevertheless. I have no heart to go further into the bloody record of the infernal institution. "Scarcely is it possible," exclaimed Antonio dei Pagliarici, "to be a Christian, and die quietly in one's bed."

Freedom of thought, indeed! Why, in the very year in which Copernicus' immortal work on the Revolutions of the Heavenly Bodies was printed (1643), Cardinal Caraffa decreed that "no book whatever, whether new or old, and whatever its contents, should, for the future, be printed without permission from the inquisitors." And this stringent regulation was applied not only to publishers and booksellers, but even private persons were required to denounce all forbidden books, to exert their utmost power to effect the destruction of all that came to their knowledge. This gradually gave rise to the Index of Prohibited Books, of which Paul Sarpi said: "Never will a more effectual means be discovered of making dunces of men, under the pretense of making them more pious." And here let me remind Archbishop Purcell that it was not until the year 1835 that the work of Copernicus was removed from the *index librorum prohibitorum*. Since that time I suppose the Romish Church allows the earth to turn on its axis and to revolve round the sun.

With what brazen effrontery does the Archbishop, in the face of all the facts of history, say that, "When men chose to use their freedom to err, the Church did not, and could not hinder them." Does he think to gloss over the foul crimes of the Church by mentioning the names of half a dozen persons whom she did *not* burn? No thanks to her, methinks, that she did not burn Luther and the rest of them.

It is the simple fact of history, without any exaggeration whatever, that the Romish Church has never, during the whole period of her history, tolerated free thought. Philosophy and science, in some sense of the terms, are an abomination to her. I need only to mention the names Abelard, Roger Bacon, Galileo, Giordano Bruno, Fenelon, Lamenais, Hermes, Guenther, Renan, to show you that through "the long lapse of ages" *the* Church does not change in this respect. Let me quote to you the words of the last philosophic victim to Romish intolerance. Frohschammer, Roman Catholic Professor of Philosophy at the University of Munich, whose books and lectures have recently been interdicted, says: "The position of a Catholic author, who is in earnest with his science, does not merely rehash the same old story, but has an eye to the needs of the age, is really pitiable. He is treated as an innovator, denounced, and, where it is possible, condemned. The work of his inspiration and toil is branded as anti-ecclesiastical, and his fellow-believers are forbidden, under pains and punishments, to read it. It is not to be wondered at when, in view of the proceedings of the Congregation of the Index, our opponents tell us, in bitter mockery, that Catholic men of learning have nothing to do but play the part of dumb dogs, and are fit for nothing but to be passive instruments of outward authority. That, under such circumstances, progress in science can not be thought of, is a matter of course." And yet Professor Frohschammer never dreamed of departing from the Catholic faith. Ah, yes, this is the "contradiction" which will yet break the Catholic Church in pieces.

Either Archbishop Purcell has learnt his lesson very badly, or he consciously uttered, last Sunday, what he knew to be untrue. This is the only alternative. As the former supposition is the most charitable, I would respectfully recommend him to study carefully the Encyclical Letter of the Pope, with its syllabus of modern errors, bearing the date of December 8th, 1861. Here he will find himself suddenly transferred to the darkest period of the middle ages. He will find that all our modern civilization is one stupendous heresy. He will find that Rome *does not pretend to tolerate free thought, or free any thing.* Does any one imagine that he is free to embrace and profess any religion which, by the light of reason, he believes to be true, or that there is any hope whatever of salvation for those who are not found within the Roman Church? Does he believe that in our day it is no longer expedient for the State to reorganize Roman Catholicism as the one true religion, to the exclusion of all other forms of worship? that the Church has no right to employ force? that in a conflict between Church and State, the law of the State is to decide? or that Church and State ought in any way to be separated? Does he think that the direction of the public schools in a Christian land must be subject to the State, and that the Roman Catholic Church has no right to interfere with the studies, discipline, or choice of teachers? Does he imagine that he has a right to circulate the Bible, or that Protestantism is only a different form of the one true Christian religion, and that a Protestant is as well-pleasing to God as a Catholic? Does he think that the method and principles, according to which the old scholastic doctors elaborated the theology of the Church, are wholly inadequate to the needs of our time or to the progress of science? Does he think that philosophy, or ethics, or civil laws, can and may deviate from the authority of the Roman Catholic Church? or, last, but not least, does he believe that the Pope of Rome can and must reconcile himself to progress and liberalism—in a word, conform to modern civilization? Then he is a child of the devil, blind and wicked to the last degree! for these are all damnable heresies, branded as such by the vicegerent of Christ, in the year of grace 1864.*

Yes, my friends, *Thought* is the one thing which the Catholic Church hates with a deadly hatred, as every institution must which imagines itself to be in the exclusive possession of the truth. And for this reason she is the most dangerous element in modern society. Wherever there is ignorance, mental and moral degradation, rottenness in the family or in the State, there she is a power, before which all the intelligence of the world may pause and tremble. She is impudent, unscrupulous, treacherous, malignant to the last degree. Oh, beware of her! beware!

And thou, dark spirit, with thy whole brood of night and hell, beware! beware! Think not to extinguish

---

* All the above-mentioned heresies are translated literally from the authorized edition of Encyclicæ, of December 8th, 1864.

the light from heaven, or to cover up the rising sun with scarlet robes or sable cassocks.

After the Albigenses come the Hussites, and requite with bloody vengeance what their brethren suffered; after Huss and Ziska follow Luther, Hutten, the war of thirty years, the Huguenots, the stormers of the Bastile, and after these the endless army of warriors for the light and truth of God.

ARCHBISHOP PURCELL'S REPLY TO REV. THOMAS VICKERS.

(Published in the *Catholic Telegraph*, October 16, 1867.)

"DESIRING to be teachers of the law, not understanding either what they say, or whereof they affirm." (1 Tim. i: 7.) The sermon preached last Sunday by Rev. Thomas Vickers, purporting to be a reply to the remarks of Archbishop Purcell, at the laying of the corner-stone of the Church of St. Rose, has been published in two, at least, of our city papers. It is a remarkable illustration of the truth of the words of St. Paul at the head of this article. That there were then, and are now, men "desiring to be teachers of the law, not understanding what they say or of what they affirm." One of these is Rev. Thomas Vickers.

Before passing to the proof, we must ask attention to the fact that Archbishop Purcell was not in this instance any more than in sundry others, the aggressor. It is Mr. Vickers who calls the Church a rotten ecclesiastical institution; it is he who qualifies her missionaries as "prize-fighters," and who consigns herself to "rats and mice." If this be not "intellectual rowdyism," to use his elegant phraseology, we know not what deserves the name. And as if this were not sufficient to show the reverend gentleman's address in the use of a theological "shillalah, his want of education and breeding," he passes over, in the very exordium of his discourse, from the ecclesiastical to the political arena, and launches the anathema of "despotism" against the freemen of the good State of Ohio, who succeeded in the last election. Is this, in the judgment of the Rev. Mr. Vickers, their reward for vindicating the right to think for themselves? Ah! ye one hundred and fifty thousand despots, beware. This new inquisitor, this modern Torquemada, will put the screws to you. It is thus he illustrates his idea of freethinking; it is thus that he hopes to escape the charge of palpable contradiction; it is thus that he seeks to distract the attention of his hearers from the point at issue between him and me. After this handsome dodge, the gentleman tells us that the old heroes of Greece and Rome, who passed a night— it was a long one of eight hundred years—in the monasteries, were no heroes at all, but only books—to which, he thus avows, the ignorant monks gave the "sanctuary" of an altar, and which, God bless them, they transcribed hundreds of times, and handed to us in the dawn of a better day, across the isthmus of the dark ages. Mr. Vickers, who, we believe, thinks he is free to deny, and does deny the Divinity, the divine and human nature of Jesus Christ, next passes to irreverence and blasphemy, using language which no Christian, and no gentleman should use: "The new dogma," says he, "of the Immaculate Conception makes Jesus the cause of his own grandmother's having brought his mother into the world without due process of nature." This language plainly shows that Rev. Mr. Vickers "does not understand that whereof he affirms." The doctrine of the

Immaculate Conception does not suppose, or teach, that Mary, the Mother of our Lord Jesus Christ, was brought into the world without due process of nature. On the contrary, it teaches that she was brought into the world as all other children are, with the exception that, as the Prophet Jeremiah and Saint John the Baptist, as the Holy Bible teaches, were sanctified in their mother's womb, so Mary was sanctified in the first moment of her conception, itself the result of the sacred process of nature. Now, dear Mr. Vickers, you do not believe in original sin; you therefore believe that you were born immaculate! Do you, therefore, believe that you were brought into the world without due process of nature? You have taken the liberty of asking me questions. Let me, for once, catechise you and direct the attention of all the churches of Cincinnati to your answer. Do you believe that "Jesus" was brought into the world without what you call "due process of nature?" If you do not believe that he was, I would not waste time by noticing you a moment longer. I have no heart to reason with those who deny the Redeemer. They may associate with Voltaire, and Strauss, and Renan, with whom I leave them free to think they shall have congenial fellowship. The gentleman proves by what he says of the so-called "Dark Ages," he is in the dark concerning them. I did not think it necessary to enumerate the bright lights that illuminated the firmament of religion and letters during the long period from the sixth to the fourteenth century. I thought better of the gentleman's scholarship, than to presume he had never heard of Hallam and Maitland, and I need not tell intelligent readers who they were, or what they have written of the mediæval era.

The Venerable Bede was born in 675. Alcuin, founder of the Palatine school, and through it, of the University of Paris, the teacher and counselor of Charlemagne, was born in the eighth century. Alfred the Great in 874; St. Bernard in 925; St. Bonaventura in 1221; Peter of Blois in the twelfth century; all of these, to whom may be added many other illustrious names, flourished in the "Dark Ages." And the Greek and Latin they understood and wrote would shame but too many of the alumni of our modern universities. But if Mr. Vickers sincerely desires to estimate aright the light or darkness of the human mind from the sixth to the fourteenth century, let him stand, as we have lately done, under the lofty arches of the grand old Cathedrals of Strasburg, of Paris, of Amiens, of Beauvais, of Chartres, of Milan, all built at that period, and ask himself who built them? Who composed those magnificent epics, those poems in stone; or, if his head become not giddy at such an elevation, let him ascend one of the lofty spires of those fine old minsters, and he will see farther into his own ignorance than a "pigmy could have seen on the shoulders of a giant." He will also conclude that the sciences are sisters, and that architecture could not have created such wonders if those sisters had not stood beside her. After this *eclaircissement* the gentleman will understand why we did not "mention any thinker from the middle of the fifth to the beginning of the thirteenth century." We could name many more than he has probably ever heard of.

The gentleman next quarrels with Tertullian, because,

forsooth, he thought there was no further need to seek for saving faith after Christ and the Gospel. Now this is precisely what we think. We believe Christ and the Gospel, and we claim not, for ourselves or others, the right to think or to believe any thing contrary to what they teach. Does Mr. Vickers? If he does, let him read the graphic description St. Paul gives (2 Timothy iii: 1) of those "who are always learning and never coming to the knowledge of the truth." Christ gave his word, his religion, his holy law for our guide. We can not put it under a bushel and go about groping for something better. For this we have neither right, nor freedom. Tertullian and all the Fathers thought so, so thinks the Catholic Church. But "Tertullian never recognized the supremacy of the Roman See."

Let him read the book of his Prescriptions, and he will change his mind. In that book Tertullian challenges certain heretics to trace their origin from any of the apostles, and he then gives a list of the *Roman Pontiffs*—links in the golden chain of truth from Peter and from Christ—saying, "let heretics pretend to any thing like this—*confingant tale quid Hæretici.*" If Tertullian fell from the truth in his later years, it was because he turned freethinker. The Church let him go his ways, but they were evil. St. Cyprian never differed in faith from the Roman Pontiff. See his admirable work *de Unitate Ecclesiæ,* on the unity of the Church. See his letters to Pope St. Stephen in prison for the faith. See the acts of his glorious martyrdom for the same faith. See what St. Augustine says of the *"falx martyrii,"* which pruned off his fault of resisting the Pope in the alleged necessity of rebaptizing such as had been baptized by heretics, in which the Christian world has since decided that Cyprian was wrong and the Pope right. And see, above all, a Protestant testimony, the four splendid articles by Dr. Nevin, in the fourth volume of the Mercersburg Review, for 1852. Do please, reverend sir, read those pages, they will do you good.

St. Augustine. We referred to him as we had to Tertullian, Cyprian and others, not for their faith, or their opinions, their liberality or illiberality, as Mr. Vickers well knows, though he dexterously affects to ignore it, but as men of extraordinary genius and learning in a Church which he falsely pretends did not allow men to think. But Augustine knew the law of the empire for the suppression of heresy; and the excesses of Arians, Donatists, Circumcellions, which provoked them and made them necessary for the safety of property and life, for the very salvation of society; and while yet appealing to those laws, he remembered how he had once been a heretic himself, and he expressed the following beautiful sentiments, which portray his true spirit: "Let those," says he, *Ep. contra Fund*, " treat you harshly who know not how hard it is to get rid of old prejudices. Let those treat you harshly who have not learned how very hard it is to purify the interior eye and render it capable of contemplating the sun of the divine truth. But as for us, we are far from this disposition toward persons who are separated from us, not by errors of their own invention, but by being entangled in those of others. We are so far from this disposition that we pray God, that in refuting the false opinions of those whom you follow, not from malice, but imprudence, he would bestow upon us that spirit of peace which feels no other emotion than charity, no other interest than that of Jesus Christ, no other wish but for your salvation."

St. Thomas Aquinas, like St. Augustine, in the fifth century, was aware of the excesses committed in the south of France by the Albigenses, the "poor men of Lyons," the Cathari, the Bulgares, whom Mosheim and the Centuriators of Magdeburg and McLane so justly denounced, and of the laws passed to restrain their violence. But in referring to the words put in his mouth, or under his pen, by Rev. Mr. Vickers, in *loc. cit.*, I find them not. The chapter, as cited, is under my eyes as I write; I shall show it to any one who chooses to see it. Aquinas does not say, "**The best way to reject a heretic is to execute him.**" **He does** not say that apostates ought to be burned **without** further ceremony. Let not Mr. Vickers trust to the easy erudition of second-hand citation. If he have not the "*ipsissima verba*" of Aquinas before him, let him come to me or send his friends. I assure them there shall not be the slightest exhibition of the "odium-theologicum" in the interview, and I shall place in their hands the "Summa."

Catholics have suffered from persecution for conscience' sake as much as non-Catholics. In Ireland the persecution has continued for upward of three hundred years to the present day. But enough has been said on this subject of persecution, and all the gross exaggerations of anti-Catholic writers, in various written and oral debates, and in our pastoral letters and lectures which are in the hands of all who care to read and be enlightened. The State, and not the Church, is to blame, as the celebrated Count *d'Maistre* has shown in his letters on the Spanish inquisition. The Popes remonstrated in certain instances against the enforcement of those severe penal laws by the State. As Thomas Aquinas says, Questio XI, Art. III, Secunda Secundæ: "Ex parte autem Ecclesiæ est Misericordia ad errantium conversionem." The part of the Church is mercy unto the conversion of the erring. And in this there is no hypocrisy, any more than a jury is a hypocrite when it hands in a verdict of murder in the first degree, but appends to it a recommendation for mercy.

The Jesuits. Who have done more for science and true philosophy than they have done? Who have carried astronomical science further and higher than they have in these our own days? Not to speak of their professors of mathematics in Europe and China, who but a Jesuit has deserved and obtained the gold medal for astronomy in the present Paris Universal Exposition? Shame on the men who know not these things, or, knowing, dare deny them. The Jesuits take no unconditional vows. They make no vow to obey in any thing contrary to the known laws of God. Hence, when they do not want to obey in what the law of God approves, the doors and windows are open, and they may leave, as Passaglia did in Rome, and as others have done in Europe and America.

Now, to show my good will and good temper, I shall answer my fortune-teller's questions—Vicker, in German, means fortune-teller—although I have answered them already in my pastoral on the Encyclical and the Syllabus of 1862—and, if I mistake not, with the approval of the Cincinnati *Gazette* which, I hope, as well as the *Commercial*, will publish what I write.

1. There is no power, human or divine, that forces a man to believe a religion, or any thing else, against his own honest, enlightened convictions. I would commit a heinous crime if I received Mr. Vickers into the Catholic Church, except he was first thoroughly convinced that it was true. And I would be guilty of an equally heinous crime if I let him continue in it and administered to him its sacraments, if he was convinced that it is not true.

2. I do not believe that the Church has any right to employ force to coerce conscience. And it is a Pope who teaches me *"non est religionis religionem cogere. Inauditum est impingere fidem cum baculo."* It is no part of religion, says Pope Gregory, quoted by Father Arthur O'Leary, to a Spanish bishop, to force religion (on any one) or to drive faith into a man with a shillalah.

3. I do not want a union of Church and State—I deprecate such a union.

4. I prefer the condition of the Church in these United States to its condition in Italy, France, Spain, Austria, Bavaria.

5. I do imagine, and I know that I have a right to circulate the Bible; and one of my first acts on reaching Cincinnati, perhaps before Mr. Vickers was born—I do not know his age—was to publish a "Votum pro pace," to put at rest forever, if I could, the stale slander that the Catholic Church was opposed to the circulation of the Holy Scriptures. I offered to subscribe fifty dollars and join the Bible Society, and place a

copy of the true Bible—Douay version—in every Catholic house, but the Bible Society declined accepting the liberal proposition.*

6. I believe that the Pope has no need to reconcile himself to progress, or true Christian evangelical liberalism, for he was never, and is not now, opposed to either.

7. I do not believe that philosopy, ethics, or civil law can deviate, without error, from the teaching of the Catholic Church. They may deviate from her authority, as they may deviate from and defy the authority of God, but in doing so they are not right. The philosophy that does this is unsound, the ethics immoral, the laws unwise and unjust.

I do not now, for the first time, give these answers to the foregoing questions; and in answering them as I have done, I am not "a child of the devil, or blind and wicked to the last degree," as Mr. Vickers, to use his own vile language, is "impudent, unscrupulous, treacherous, malignant" enough to say I am. Deluded man! false teacher! I pity him, forgive him, and pray for his conversion!

J. B. PURCELL,
Archbishop of Cincinnati.

---

* Before the German Bible of Luther, and the French edition of Olivet, a Huguenot, both published in 1535, the Catholics had already translated the Bible into almost all the European languages. They had sent forth twenty-one editions of the Bible in Italian; sixteen in German; thirteen in French; ten in Flemish; five in Saxon; two in Bohemian; and four in Swiss, beside a countless number of editions in Latin, then almost the common language. See *Catholic Telegraph*, July 14, 1832.

REPLY OF REV. THOMAS VICKERS TO ARCHBISHOP PURCELL.

(Published in the Cincinnati *Gazette*, October 26, 1867.)

To the Editor of the Cincinnati Gazette:

HAVING just returned to the city after an absence of a week, I find that Archbishop Purcell has again attacked me, and in a manner even more characteristic of the Romish Church than in the first instance. I am not at all surprised that he now wishes to make it appear that he was not the aggressor. But I have no apprehension that any fair-minded man who read the wholly *impersonal* remarks which I made at the laying of the corner-stone of St. John's Church, and also the coarse, *personal* attack which the Archbishop made upon me in consequence thereof, will be deceived for a moment as to the real state of the case. Nor do I think that any man of common sense will be likely to be misled by that fine stroke of archiepiscopal dialectics in which he tries to make it appear that I am opposed to "the freemen of the good State of Ohio" thinking for themselves and acting on their thought. Is it any infraction of their "right to think for themselves" that I think differently, and say so? The manner in which the Romish Church, through such minions as Torquemada, "put the screws" to those who differed from her, was somewhat different, I take it. Was it not, most reverend sir, to use your own elegant language, a "handsome dodge" to confound the two?

THE IMMACULATE CONCEPTION.

What I said of the dogma of the Immaculate Conception was simply intended to show that, in regard to the Greek and Roman philosophers, etc., the Archbishop either did not understand what I meant, or had committed the *hysteron proteron*—the logical and chronological blunder of supposing them to have been educated by men who lived ages after them—just as the new dogma supposes Mary herself to have been conceived without sin on account of the merits of a son she was to bear in the future ("*intuitu meritorum Christi Jesu*"). If the Archbishop means to assert that being conceived without sin is something *not* outside of the "due process of nature," then I am at a loss to know why he makes such a fuss about it.

THE NATURE OF JESUS.

The Archbishop wishes to catechise me, and directs "the attention of all the churches of Cincinnati" to my answer. Well, I have no objection. If I understand his question, he means to ask me whether I believe that Jesus "*was brought into the world as all other children are?*" I answer: Yes. Jesus was a man, and *as such* he is the dearest possession of humanity. The "Christ" is a theological fiction—mankind needs no *such* Redeemer as the Church has fabricated. This is my honest and sacred conviction, and I respectfully submit to the Archbishop, and to the public, that when, on this ground, he declines all further intercourse with me, he is only furnishing voluntary proof of my original thesis, viz.: That the Church never tolerates any body who differs from her; that free thought (which means nothing without the liberty to express it) is an abomination to her.

THE POINT AT ISSUE.

And it is this thesis of which I wish to remind the Archbishop. It was the assertion, that the Church had never tolerated free thought, which he attempted in his first animadversion, to prove untrue; and for this express purpose that he quoted the array of names so fatal to his argument. He referred to them not merely "as men of extraordinary genius and learning," as he now pretends, but as illustrations of free thought within the pale of the Church. Of course, it was a sad fact for the Archbishop that, on examination, not one of them answered to his description; that those of them who took the liberty of thinking for themselves lost favor with the Church; and those who retained her favor, so far from being illustrations, were the bitter opponents of free thought. Stick to the point at issue, if you please.

DARK AGES AND CATHEDRALS.

I am happy to inform the Archbishop that I am not dependent for my knowledge of mediæval history and literature on either Hallam or Maitland, although I am not ignorant of what they have written. But to what purpose is the new list of names with which he favors us? Was free thought better "illustrated" and more fully "exercised" by Bede, Alcuin, Alfred the Great,

St. Bernard, Bonaventura, and Peter of Blois, than by the eight persons he first mentioned? This is the point. Let him have done with the " easy erudition " of looking into Hallam or Maitland and culling out a few high-sounding names in order to impose upon the unlearned. Furthermore, there is certainly no objection to the Archbishop making it known to the community that he has recently stood under the arches of certain ancient cathedrals, but the public will doubtless be at a loss to know what that fact, or what the cathedrals any way have to do with the subject under discussion. Do the six cathedrals he mentions, any more than the six new names he has brought forward, prove that the Church tolerates free thought? What has the sisterhood of the *sciences* to do with the building of cathedrals? Keep to the point, if you please.

TERTULLIAN.

The Archbishop admits, substantially, what I asserted in regard to Tertullian, except on one point. I asserted that " he never recognized the supremacy of the Roman Bishop." The Archbishop tells me to read " the book of his Prescriptions," and I shall change my mind. Now, I am not in this instance going to doubt either the honesty or scholarship of the Archbishop, (I shall come to a more glaring case by and by,) but simply to state facts. Not only does Tertullian in his book *De pudicitia* use the most contemptuous language concerning the Roman bishop, but there is not in the whole book, *De præscriptionibus hæreticorum* (to which the Archbishop refers) a single word which, taken in the connection in which it occurs, even looks like acknowledging the Roman supremacy; while, on the other hand, there are plenty of passages which show conclusively that he never dreamed of acknowledging it. So much for Tertullian.

CYPRIAN.

The Archbishop says Cyprian "never differed in faith from the Roman Pontiff." Now, if he means by the word "Pontiff" any thing more than "bishop," it is perfectly clear that nobody could differ from him in any thing, for, *in Cyprian's time, there was no such thing as a Roman Pontiff*—that was a later growth. But I never said that Cyprian differed "in faith" from the Roman bishop. I simply said that Stephen excommunicated him for venturing to have and express an opinion different from his own.

And I now say that the result of the controversy on the validity of baptism by heretics proved not only that Cyprian did not recognize the supremacy of Rome, but that the whole African Church and all the Asiatic bishops resisted the arrogance of Stephen. There is still extant a letter to Cyprian, written in the name of the Asiatic bishops, by Firmilian, Bishop of Cæsarea, in which he can scarcely find language forcible enough to express his contempt for the Roman authority. The man whom the Archbishop calls "Pope St. Stephen," Firmilian (his brother bishop) compares to Judas; speaks of his audacity and insolence; says he is justly indignant at his open and manifest stupidity (*juste indignor ad hanc tam apertam et manifestam Stephani stultitiam*), and calls him the slanderer of the blessed apostles Peter and Paul (*infamans Petrum et Paulum beatos*

Apostolos). It will be seen from the following passage in what light the assumed power of the Roman bishop to excommunicate other bishops was regarded in those days: "What grievous sin hast thou committed in separating thyself from so many flocks! Thou hast cut off thyself; be not deceived, for he is truly a schismatic who has made himself an apostate from the communion of ecclesiastical unity. For, while imagining that thou hast excommunicated all others, thou hast in reality excommunicated thyself alone." This I translate literally from the original, and beg the reader to remember that the words are addressed to "Pope St. Stephen!" Perhaps the Archbishop may not consider Firmilian as good authority as Rev. Dr. Nevin.

AUGUSTINE.

I asserted that Augustine was the first of the Fathers to elaborate a theory for compulsion and persecution in matters of religion, and that he is to-day the great authority to which the Romish Church looks for her right to punish heretics. My opponent does not, and can not with truth, deny this, but he seeks to evade it by putting the character of Augustine in a false light. Now, either Archbishop Purcell knows that the "*Liber contra epistolam Manichæi, quam dicunt fundamenti,*" (which is the meaning of his bungling citation: "*Ep. contra fund,*")—he either knows that this book, from which he makes his garbled extract, was written *long before* the Donatist controversy, during which (as I stated) Augustine elaborated his brutal theory of compulsion and persecution from the text, Luke xiv: 23, and, therefore, proves nothing but that his originally mild disposition toward heretics became bitter and vindictive in his later years, or he is not aware of this simple fact of history. In the one case he has knowledge of a fact which he tries to conceal from his readers; in the other, his ignorance proves that he has no claim to be heard in the matter. Which horn of the dilemma will the Archbishop take? Will he sacrifice his scholarship or his honesty? And now for

THOMAS AQUINAS.

Here I must confess that when I read the Archbishop's paragraph, I could scarcely believe my senses. I had asserted that Aquinas was one of the defenders of the right of the Church to use violence against heretics; that he advocated putting them to death "after the first and second admonition," and taught that apostates were to be executed without further ceremony. I did not pretend to give the exact words; I gave the sense, and quoted the paragraphs of the "Summa," in which this doctrine is contained, so that whoever desired, and had the opportunity, could refer to them and verify my statement. Now the Archbishop comes and seeks to give the public the impression that I relied on the "easy erudition of a second-hand citation," did not know what I was talking about, and that Aquinas had never said any such thing. He says he has "the chapter as cited under his eyes as he writes," and there is no such thing there. What am I to conclude? That, although having the book before him, he does not understand the language in which it is written? or, that he has the book, can read it, but wishes to deceive his readers as to its contents? He knew very well that no one of them would come to him to see it. Why did he not print the paragraphs in question, with a correct translation, so that his readers could judge for themselves? He was writing for a paper which bears his name as chief editor, over which he has complete control—a paper expressly devoted to the interest of the Romish Church—and was not, therefore, cramped for room. Why did he not do it? *He dared not.* He knew that, if he did, his case was irrecoverably lost. Ah, yes! dear Archbishop, I also have the "*ipsissima verba*" before me as I write, and I hope that you will not regard it as an "exhibition of the *odium theologicum*" if I print them with a translation. The following passages are found in the *Summa*, Migne's (Catholic) edition, as correctly cited in my sermon. (*Summæ Secunda Secundæ, Quæst.* XI, Art. III, IV.)

Art. III is headed: *Utrum hæretici sint tolerandi?* (Whether heretics are to be tolerated?) The method of Aquinas is first to state and meet objections, and then to develop his own opinion. Here he first cites various passages from the New Testament (2 Tim. ii: 24–26; 1 Cor. xi: 19; Matt. xiii: the parable of the tares), in favor of the opinion that heretics ought to be tolerated; to all these he opposes the passage (Tit. iii: 10, 11): "A man that is an heretic, reject," etc., and then uses the following words:

ORIGINAL.	TRANSLATION.
Respondeo dicendum quod circa hæreticos duo sunt consideranda: unum quidem ex parte ipsorum; aliud vero ex parte Ecclesiæ. Ex parte quidem ipsorum est peccatum, per quod meruerunt non so-	I reply that, in regard to heretics, there are two things to be considered: one, indeed, concerns themselves; the other surely concerns the Church. For their part they have com-

lum ab Ecclesia per excommunicationem separari, sed etiam PER MORTEM A MUNDO EXCLUDI. *Multo enim gravius est corrumpere fidem, per quam est animæ vita, quam falsare pecuniam, per quam temporali vitæ subvenitur. Unde si falsarii pecuniæ vel alii malefactores statim per seculares principes juste morti traduntur, multo magis* HÆRETICI STATIM EX QUO DE HÆRESI CONVINCUNTUR, POSSUNT NON SOLUM EXCOMMUNICARI, SED ET JUSTE OCCIDI.

mitted a sin, on account of which they not only deserve to be severed from the Church, by excommunication, *but to be removed from the world by death;* for it is a more grievous offense to corrupt the faith, which is the life of the soul, than to counterfeit money, which only helps sustain the life of the body. Hence, if counterfeiters of money, or other malefactors, are by the secular authorities, *much* justly put straightway to death *more may heretics, the instant they are convicted of heresy, not only be excommunicated, but justly killed.*

(Now follow the words, "The part of the Church is mercy to the erring," which Archbishop Purcell dishonestly tears out of their connection, in order to bind his readers.)

Ex parte autem Ecclesiæ est misericordia ad errantium conversionem; et ideo non STATIM *condemnat, sed post primam et secundam correptionem, ut Apostolus docet;* POSTMODUM *vero si adhuc pertinax inveniatur, Ecclesia de ejus conversione non sperans, aliorum saluti providet, eum ab Ecclesia separando per excommunicationis sententiam; et* ULTERIUS *relinquit eum judicio seculari* A MUNDO EXTERMINANDUM.

But the part of the Church is mercy to the erring; and, therefore, she does not *immediately* condemn, but "after the first and second admonition," as the Apostle teaches; but *afterward,* if he still be found unyielding, the Church, having no hope of his conversion, cares for the salvation of others by severing him from the Church by the sentence of excommunication; and *finally* delivers him over to the secular tribunal *to be exterminated from the world by death!*

The following is the heading of Art. IV: *Utrum revertentes ab hæresi sint ab Ecclesia recipiendi?* (Whether those who renounce their heresy are to be received by the Church?) Aquinas follows the same method here, first stating the reasons of the opposite side, and then refuting them. His own conclusion is contained in the following extract:

ORIGINAL.	TRANSLATION.
Et ideo Ecclesia primo quidem, revertentes ab hæresi, non solum recipit ad pœnitentiam, sed etiam conservat eos in vita, et interdum restituit eos dispensative ad ecclesiasticas dignitates quas primus habebant, si videantur vere conversi; et hoc pro bono pacis frequenter legitur esse factum. Sed quando recepti iterum relabuntur; videtur esse signum inconstantiæ eorum circa fidem; et ideo ulterius redeuntes recipiuntur quidem ad pœnitentiam, NON TAMEN UN LIBERENTUR A SENTENTIA MORTIS.	And, therefore, the Church, in the first instance, not only admits to penitence those who renounce their heresy, but she also preserves their lives, and occasionally restores them, by dispensation, to their former ecclesiastical honors, when they appear to be truly converted; and this, for the sake of peace, is frequently taken for granted; but when those who have been restored again relapse, it seems to be a sign of their inconstancy in faith, and, therefore, such as afterward return are indeed admitted to penitence, *but not liberated from the sentence of death.*

"God," continues Aquinas, "who is the searcher of hearts, knows whether those who return are sincere, always receives them; but the Church can not imitate Him, for it is to be presumed that those were not really converted, who, having been received, fell again; and, therefore, while she does not deny them the means of salvation, she refuses to save them from impending death" (*periculo mortis eos non tuetur*).

Now, in this book, Thomas Aquinas is not writing a polemic treatise against "the Albigenses, the 'poor men of Lyons,' the Cathari, the Bulgares," or any other special class of heretics, but he is writing a body of Christian doctrine, universally true, and universally applicable, and which the Romish Church to-day adopts as a standard. I dare not trust myself to characterize, in fitting language, this attempt of Archbishop Purcell to defend a bad cause by such reprehensible means. The public is now in possession of the evidence, and will give its own verdict.

THE JESUITS.

After the above exposition, our confidence in what the Archbishop says will not be very great. When he affirms that "the Jesuits take no unconditional vows;" that "they make no vow to obey in any thing contrary to the known laws of God;" I beg leave to refer him to the text of the Constitution of the Society of Jesus, where he will find the following words: The candidate "*must regard the Superior as* CHRIST THE LORD, and must strive to acquire perfect resignation and denial of his own will and judgment, *in all things* conforming his will and judgment to that which the Superior wills and judges" (Const., par. iii, cap. i, sec. 23). And also the following: "As for holy obedience, this virtue must be perfect in every point—in execution, in will, in intellect—doing what is enjoined with all celerity, spiritual joy, and perseverance; *persuading ourself that every thing is just;* suppressing every repugnant thought and judgment of one's own in a certain obedience; . . . . . and let every one persuade himself that he who lives under obedience should be moved and directed, under Divine Providence, by his Superior, *just as if he were a corpse (perinde ac si cadaver esset)*, which allows itself to be moved and led in any direction" (Const., par. vi, cap. i, sec. 1).

THE POPE'S SYLLABUS *vs.* THE ARCHBISHOP'S.

In conclusion, I can not but congratulate the Archbishop on his syllabus of answers to my questions. In some respects he is decidedly in advance of his master, the Pope; nay, he is a rank heretic, and, as such, is in great danger of being excommunicated, and perhaps burned. Let us see what the Pope says, on the one hand, and the Archbishop, on the other. I translate from the authorized edition of the *Litteræ Encyclycæ:*

THE POPE.	THE ARCHBISHOP.
1. It is a damnable error to maintain that "every man is free to embrace and profess that religion which his reason leads him to believe to be true." (§ III, XV.)	1. "There is no power, human or divine, that forces a man to believe a religion, or any thing else, against his own honest, enlightened convictions."
2. It is a damnable error to maintain that "the Church ought to be separated from the State, and the State from the Church." (§ VII, LV.)	2. "I do not want a union of Church and State; I deprecate such a Union."
3. The Pope calls Bible Societies "pestilences," and says he has often condemned them in the severest language. (§ IV.)	3. The Archbishop says he proposed to join the Bible Society, and help to circulate the Bible.

I think the question will occur to every one, which represents the Romish Church: the Pope, or the Archbishop of Cincinnati?

In conclusion, let me correct another misstatement of the Archbishop's. He asserted that I called him "impudent, unscrupulous, treacherous, malignant." I never did such a thing, as every one knows who read my sermon. I will not say what I think about it now. Facts speak for themselves.

THOMAS VICKERS,
Minister of the First Congregational Society.

ARCHBISHOP PURCELL'S REPLY TO REV. THOMAS VICKERS.

(Published in the *Catholic Telegraph*, October 30, 1867.)

"Thomas Vickers, minister of the First Congregational Society"—he does not say where—occupies more than a column of the Cincinnati *Gazette*, of the 26th October, in which, in the vain effort to extricate himself from the mire of his former flounderings, he sinks more irretrievably.

In one of those efforts he endeavored to entertain the worshipers in Hopkins' Hall with the irreverent information that "Jesus, by an anticipated application of the merits of the atonement, made his grandmother bring his mother into the world without due process of nature." We argued, that if Mary, in virtue of her immaculate conception, or exemption from original sin, which is the same thing, was born without due process of nature, then Mr. Vickers, who believes not in original sin, and who, therefore, believes that he was conceived immaculate, was brought into the world without due process of nature. To this inexorable "*argumentum ad hominem*," he has taken care, after a week's reflection, not to answer. Perhaps in his next he will tell the First Congregational Society how he came into the world at all, and how he came to be their minister.

He also insists in the paper before us, that when he branded the freemen of Ohio, "despots," he inflicted on them no censure, insinuated no reproach. Then why did he so brand them?

When the gentleman says that "Christ is a theological fiction," and not God, we solemnly declare that such blasphemous freethinking is an abomination to the Church and to us, and should be such to every Christian—at the same time that we would not for the world abridge Mr. Vickers of his freedom to think and to speak as he does to all who pay him for such thinking and such speaking!

We said that thought is essentially free, that neither God nor the Church could enslave it. And this, we still contend, is true. Men could think and speak as they pleased, but when they thought and spoke what was wrong, the Church had the right to tell them so, as Mr. Vickers now tells the "despots" of Ohio. Stick to the point, sir!

The gentleman returns to the "Dark Ages," to prove that they were dark, and that the Church made them dark—that she put an extinguisher on the human mind by not tolerating "freethinking." Is not this the point, friend? Now we could occupy all the columns of one number of the *Gazette* or *Commercial* with extracts from non-Catholic writers, leaving out Maitland and Hallam, to prove that they were ages of light and not of darkness in the sense of Mr. Vickers, and that we are indebted to them for the greater measure of light that we enjoy. A Catholic churchman he would not believe on this subject. Here is testimony to which he may not demur. It is that of a radical Unitarian left wing—

namely, Ralph Waldo Emerson, in an oration delivered by him at Harvard College.

"In modern Europe, the middle ages were called the 'Dark Ages,' ten centuries, from the fifth to the fifteenth. Who dares to call them so now? They are seen to be the feet on which we walk, the eyes with which we see. They gave us decimal numbers, gunpowder, glass, chemistry, and Gothic architecture, and their paintings ever the delight and tuition of our age. Six centuries ago Roger Bacon explained the Procession of the Equinoxes, and looking over the horizon from London to America, announced that ships could be constructed that could be driven more rapidly than a whole galley of rowers could drive them, and machines which could fly into the air like birds."

"They also," adds the author, or reporter of this oration, "gave us the discovery of America and the invention of the art of printing. The darkness of those times arises from our own want of information, not from the absence of intelligence that distinguished them. Human thought was never more active and never produced greater results in any period of the world."

In some sense, as even Carlyle admits, (see "The Hero and Poet," page 129, U. P. James, Cincinnati, 1842): "This glorious Elizabethan era, with its Shakspeare as the outcome and flowerage of all which had preceded it, is itself attributable to the Catholicism of the middle ages. The Christian faith, which was the theme of Dante's song, had produced the practical life which Shakspeare was to sing. For religion, then, as it is now and always is, was the soul of practice—the primary vital fact in men's life." Your flowerage, Mr.

Vickers, and that of all who think like you, your flowerage, who forget what you owe to a Catholic ancestry is—poppy.

Mr. Vickers introduces a new name when he cites Firmilian. But in this he flounders in the mire again. For if it were true that Firmilian used the coarse language in addressing the martyred Pope, St. Stephen, which Mr. Vickers quotes, it would only prove what we told him before, that *de jure et de facto* the Church could not, and did not, interdict free thought. But if the gentleman reads the dissertation in 4to, written by Marcellinus Molkenbuhr, and printed in Munster, Westphalia, in 1790, he will find that the letter in question was falsely attributed to Firmilian, and that it was, on the contrary, the production of an African Donatist of the fourth century.

Tertullian eloquently defended the Catholic faith, and showed its purity maintained by Peter, whom Christ made the head of his Church on earth, and Peter's successors in the See of Rome; and when, by undue harshness to the erring, he forfeited charity, he became a Montanist, and then thought and wrote as freely as he pleased, *de pudicitia*, or any thing else.

Augustine and Aquinas knew the laws in force in their respective ages against heresy, which the civil power, like the Scripture classed with the most heinous crimes: "idolatry, enmities, quarrels, dissensions, sects, envyings, murders, drunkenness—of the which I foretell you that they who do such things shall not obtain the kingdom of God." (St Paul's Ep. to Gal., vs. 20, 21.) The very text of Aquinas, as quoted by Mr. Vickers, was quoted by Archbishop Purcell. The author of the

Summa did say, as Mr. Vickers acknowledges, that the part of the Church was mercy, but that when the heretic continued obstinate, she had nothing more to do in his case, but leave him to the State—"*Ulterius relinquit eum judici seculari a mundo exterminandum.*" With this consummation the Church had no more to do than she had to do with Jehovah's laws against false religions under the old dispensation. In this she had no more to do in suppressing free thought than God had when he thundered from Sinai: "Thou shalt not covet." In this the Archbishop suppressed nothing—had nothing to suppress; had no need of reticence, and concealed nothing. But he could scarcely believe his senses when Mr. Vickers, with the hope of helping his cause by horrifying his readers, spoke of *flames* and *burning*, not a word of which is to be found in the text which he pretends to quote so ingenuously from St. Thomas. But if, in a by-gone age, Aquinas, or any one else, a thousand times over justified the punishment of death for heresy, it is no more than has been done almost in our own age, "down East;" and as, thank God! the world has outgrown the policy and practice which we now so cordially condemn here in the United States, where Catholics were the first to proclaim liberty of conscience for all, it is with a bad grace, indeed, that a Unitarian rakes up the buried embers of the New England witches, or the long-extinguished fires of scriptural or mediæval persecution for conscience' sake.

In Archbishop Purcell's Pastoral on the Syllabus, in 1862, he used language similar to that of his answer to Mr. Vickers; and he has since stood in the near presence of His Holiness, and of five hundred of his brother bishops, and has not been rebuked for his recorded sentiments and avowed convictions by him or them. We Catholics know our religion, and have not to learn it from enemies, who, like the pagan tyrant of old, dressed the Christians in the skins of wild beasts, and then set the dogs on them.

It is disingenuous, dishonest in Mr. Vickers to take no notice of the answers given to his calumnious imputations. If it were another man than one appearing in the garb of a "minister," we might be tempted to use a monosyllable, when he says an indulgence is a pardon for past or a license for future sin—that the Catholic Church is opposed to the circulation of the Bible, or that the Jesuits' vow binds them to any thing contrary to the known law of God. In conclusion, as the gentleman can hardly open his mouth without making a misstatement, we tell him that Archbishop Purcell is not the editor of the *Catholic Telegraph*, whatever control he may exercise over its columns.

For the information of all who sincerely seek the truth on questions started by Rev. Mr. Vickers, who seems comfortably ignorant of the past, as if he had spent his life in a cave, or had slept an age, like Rip Van Winkle, we publish all our Pastoral of 1865:

Venerable Brethren of the Clergy;
Beloved Brethren of the Laity:

ON the memorable and ever glorious Festival of Pentecost, 1862, when the Catholicity of the true Church was illustrated in a manner never previously witnessed in her eventful history; when three hundred bishops, many of whom had come from Lands and Sees whose names would be sought in vain in the annals of the General Councils, surrounded the Holy Father in that "Eternal ark of worship undefiled," which, "of Temples old and altars new, standeth alone with nothing like to it," the mind of the Vicar of CHRIST was preoccupied with the thought of the monstrous errors which were undermining the very foundations of social and religious order, and threatening to banish the fear and the love, the name and the idea, of God from the Universe. Faithful to the office committed to him by the Prince of Pastors, to guard his lambs and sheep from prowling wolves, to lead them to wholesome pastures and refreshing streams, the Supreme Pontiff commanded that a syllabus, or list, of the most perverse and dangerous of these errors should be communicated to us, and, doubtless, to every one of the assembled Prelates, to be thoughtfully, conscientiously, prayerfully considered by us, with the aid of such member of our clergy as we deemed most capable, for learning, prudence and piety, to assist us in their examination, censure and correction.

When "PETER spoke, the much disputing ceased" in the first, the model, Council of Jerusalem. The voice of the successor of PETER was heard in the subsequent Councils, as the voice of God. When he spoke, the cause was ended. His decrees are irreformable, his judgment irreversible, his verdict infallible. Nevertheless, with the humility of Him who asked His Apostles "who did men say, who did *they* say that He was," the Pope, who "lords it not over our faith," condescends to ask and patiently awaits the answers of his brethren, from June, 1862, to December, 1864, before pronouncing a definitive judgment.

This judgment has been pronounced, this sentence proclaimed to the world in the Encyclical, or Circular, of the 8th December, the ninth anniversary of the Declaration of the Dogma of the Immaculate Conception. We bow to it reverently; we receive it implicitly; we embrace it cordially; we hail it gratefully. To us it is as the voice of God on Sinai, on the Jordan, on Thabor.

"Why is it not so received by all?" To whom else have been entrusted "the words of eternal life?" For whom else has CHRIST prayed "that his faith may never fail?" To whom else has He given the charge to confirm "his brethren." By whom else has he ever drawn a single nation from Paganism to Christianity? Whom else did he make the civilizer of barbarians? Whom else, according to even infidel authority, did He make, "politically, socially, and morally, the savior of Europe?" By whom else did He have "the effort made, commensurate with the danger, that saved Europe from Islamism, and prevented the evidences of the Koran from being demonstrated to a circumcised audience in the halls of Oxford?"

We are bound to remind men of these cardinal truths of history, when they make it convenient to forget them. We are bound to set up those landmarks, when men, from sinister motives, cast them down.

We are aware that the Pope showed little worldly wisdom when he issued the Encyclical. It was neither a homage to Cæsarism, nor a bid for popularity. But he occupies high and holy ground. His stand was on the watch-tower, where CHRIST had placed him, and where he beheld from afar the rolling up of the dark, portentous clouds, where he heard the first mutterings of the storm, of which the world at his feet, immersed in sensual and ambitious projects, seemed utterly unconscious, and he gave to all the solemn warning, like the unheeded Noah of old, to fly from the wrath to come, to seek shelter and safety in the ark.

The docile children of the Church could have desired that copies of the Encyclical had been sent to them, to be translated, before they had been misinterpreted and perverted by anti-Catholic and infidel journalists. Had this been done, the hue and cry that greeted its appearance might have been less violent. But in this, too, we recognize the hand of Providence sweetly and strongly disposing all things. Suspecting no evil, we left the important document in the hands of the manufacturers of public opinion for two Continents, the London *Times* and Paris *Siecle* and its compeers; and never was ignorance more gross, or bad faith more barefaced and unblushing, than are betrayed in their translation of, and comments on, the Encyclical. The Editor of the *Times* is now impaled on the horns of the "mad bull" of his own creation; and the illustrious Bishop DUPANLOUP, of Orleans, has exhibited the infidel press of the French capital in a condition not less humiliating, or more enviable. We have published this noble Prelate's work in the columns of the Catholic TELEGRAPH and WAHRHEITSFREUND, and in pamphlet form, so that all, who will, may read and understand the perfidy of the Convention of the 15th September, and the true import of the Encyclical. The Pope has solemnly approved the writing of the Bishop of Orleans; the Cardinal Vicar, PATRIZI, has approved it; the Cardinal Secretary of State, ANTONELLI, has approved it. The silence, the humiliation, of the enemies of the truth, the Pope and the Church have, in their way, approved it. The many-headed hydra, the multifarious errors, of the condemned propositions, crushed by a mightier club than that of the mythological HERCULES, have approved it by their death screams.

But let us hear an able vindication of the Pope and the Encyclical from another, a non-Catholic, source. It is the Berlin *Review* that now speaks:

"When an old, helpless captive, a plundered man,
"whom God has ordained to be the judge and the ex-
"ecutor of the laws of heaven, becomes the accuser,
"when to States become godless he recalls the remem-
"brance of those doctrines which alone give duration
"to nations and power, it is a sign that the wave of
"worldly success has reached its highest tide, that the
"reaction has begun which will show how empty and
"how short-lived are selfish triumphs. The laurel of
"the conqueror fades, and the unarmed is victor. . . .
"The Lieutenancy of Pope PIUS IX will fill a glorious
"place in the history of Catholic Christendom. It is
"undeniable that under this Pope, Catholicism has made
"greater conquests than for centuries past. The bold
"decree by which PIUS districted England into dioceses,
"and sent to Westminster an Archbishop who should
"gather the sons of the faithful, and win back the fallen,
"was a deed of conquest. The raising of the Immacu-
"late Conception of MARY to an undoubted Dogma of
"the Church, served as evidence that Catholicism, in
"matters of Christian faith, was still full of vigorous
"action. Finally, the martyrium of PIUS IX has put
"the seal to the plenitude of life in his Church.

"Religious doubt and State tyranny go hand in hand. "The human mind, which the arrogance of emancipated "science flings from one uncertainty to another, at last "surrenders to the thesis that wealth and pleasure are "the only goods for man; and thus arises the moral "anarchy in which every individual must bend to the "pressure of the strongest usurper. From this corrup-"tion Pius saves his Christian flock by the healing power "of authority in faith.

"Therefore the Emperor trembles. He wanted to "storm heaven, and forgot that man is great then only "when he confesses that he is less than heaven. 'Cœlum "debellet Imperator,' says Tertullian, 'cœlum capti-"'vum triumpho suo invehat. Non potest. Ideo mag-"'nus est quia cœlo minor est.' And Pius IX eluci-"dated the warning of Tertullian, when a few days "ago he addressed to the French General, 'Justice and "'judgment are the preparation of thy seat.' He who "holds a place to which he has no right, will be judged "and cast off by the Redeemer. . . . No, the warn-"ing of the Pope is a progress-favoring counter stroke "against immersion in the swamp into which Imperial "skepticism would have plunged us. . . . We are "to be sent in pursuit of the false and the frivolous: but "the Church puts a stop to the fool's chase by teaching "us that we find rest in submission to the authority of "faith and the redeeming Son of God."

Let us now look at the condemned propositions, and see if we can not assent to the justice, and wisdom, and necessity of their condemnation with the same full-ness of faith and the same conviction of the under-standing with which the first Christians received the

Four Gospels, the early Fathers subscribed to the first four General Councils, and their children and successors in the faith, in these latter ages, the decisions of Trent and the Creed of Pope Pius IV.

We do not believe in the absurdity of Pantheism— that every thing in the Universe is an integral part of GOD—and that there is no other, no personal GOD. We do not believe that every thing made itself and made every thing else. We believe that there is a personal GOD, who made all that exists; that the hyena, the demon, the assassin is not any part of GOD, and if he were, we would not be any part of him. Therefore, with the Encyclical, we condemn Pantheism.

We do not believe that the best form of society and the exigencies of civil progress absolutely require human society to be constituted and governed without any regard whatever to religion.

We do not believe that while GOD leaves all men free before the final judgment, to believe falsehood and do wrong, that he grants any man a *right* to believe error or to commit crime. We do not believe that in this sense liberty of conscience and of worship is the right of any man, which should be proclaimed by law, and that citizens should have the right to all kinds of liberty, to be restrained by no law, Ecclesiastical or Civil, by which they may be enabled to manifest openly and publicly their ideas by word of mouth, through the press, or any other means. The maxim that error may be left free to write or speak what it pleases, as long as truth is left free to combat it, has been illustrated by the penalties incurred by those who dared, recently, to speak and write against the Union and the Constitution, and to recommend assassination and sympathize with assassins.

We do not believe that the will of the people, manifested by what is called public opinion, or in any other way, constitutes the supreme law, independent of all divine and human right; and that in the political order, accomplished facts, by the mere fact of having been accomplished, have the force of right. He that by chicanery, knavery, or force, robs me of houses or lands, is as much a thief as he who steals my purse. Length of unjust possession confers no right, and the land and the money robber are equally bound to restitution of principal and interest.

When we rise from the reading of SPELMAN's History of Sacrilege in England, we do not believe that the suppression of the Monasteries, the spoliation of shrines, the seizing of the rich domains, into which drained swamps, reclaimed wastes, and cleared forests were changed by the toil of the Monks, have been left wholly unpunished by divine justice even in this world; or that they will be more leniently dealt with in the next; and, therefore, we can not believe, against the dictates of reason, justice, and humanity, that the Encyclical is wrong in denouncing the imitation of such sacrilege in Piedmont, Portugal, Spain, or any other country.

We do not believe that "property is robbery;" that a new division of whatever a toiling man has earned during the week should be made with his lazy, drunken, gambling neighbor every Saturday night.

We do not believe that civil law has a right to abolish the Sabbath, or the religious holiday; that it has the right to grant divorces from the bond of marriage—that is, to do what CHRIST has forbidden, "separate "those whom GOD has joined together."

We do not believe, with socialists and communists, that families must be absorbed by the State, that parents have not the control of their children's minds and morals—their education, except as given them by the civil law, which, by such usurpation, invades not only the dearest rights of parents, but the authority of GOD Himself, delegated to these His representatives on earth.

We do not believe that the Clergy have ever been the enemies of the useful sciences, of progress, or of civilization; or that they should be deprived of all participation in the work of teaching and training the young.

We do not believe that the laws of the Church do not bind the conscience if they are not promulgated by the civil power. On the contrary, as AMBROSE, the great Archbishop of Milan, the immortal ATHANASIUS, and the President of the First Council of Nice, said to contemporary kings: "The Church belongs to GOD, there-"fore, it should not be delivered up to CÆSAR. A "good Emperor is within the Church, not above it. . . . "Meddle not with Ecclesiastical matters, nor dictate to "us on such matters, but rather learn these things of "us. To you GOD has committed the Imperial sway, "to us he has entrusted what appertains to the Church. "You have no power, O, Emperor, over incense and "the sacred things." Hence, we do not believe that any earthly ruler has been made head of CHRIST's Church. Neither a Henry VIII, nor any of his successors; neither a BONAPARTE nor a VICTOR EMANUEL. Nor do we believe that that is a "Holy Synod" which professes that the HOLY GHOST is sent to it in a dispatch from the autocrat of all the Russias, in the portfolio of a colonel of huzzars!

We believe that the Church was founded by JESUS CHRIST, the Son of GOD, to guide us in all truth. That she is the ark of safety to all who will not perish; that she is supreme in spirituals.

We do not believe that all action of GOD upon man and the world is to be denied; that human reason, without regard to GOD, is the arbiter of truth and falsehood, and of good and evil, and sufficient, by its natural force, to secure the welfare of men and nations; that Christian faith is in opposition to human reason; that the prophecies and miracles recorded in the sacred Scriptures are the fictions of poets; that one religion is as good as another, unless in the sense as some said that it is, and a great deal better; that we may entertain a well-founded hope that those *who are in no manner in the true Church* (not even in desire) may be saved.

We do not believe that the abolition of the temporal powers, of which the Apostolic See is possessed, would contribute to the liberty and prosperity of the Church. The possession of temporal power of territory, is not essential to the exercise of the supreme spiritual prerogative granted by CHRIST to His Vicar. But it is convenient, it is salutary, it is sanctioned by the experience of a thousand years; and the States of the Church, even before the spoliation of the Legations, were so small that they should never have attempted the cupidity of the sacrilegious invader.

We do not believe that the Roman Pontiff can and

ought to reconcile himself to and agree with progress, liberalism, and civilization; for he has never quarreled with true progress, true liberty, or Christian civilization, in the front ranks of which he has been ever seen since the very origin of Christianity.

We do not believe that the civil authority possesses power to decide, in the matter of administering the Divine Sacraments, as to the dispositions necessary for their reception.

We do not believe that the savage is better than the Christian and civilized condition of society; that naturalism is preferable to revelation; or that reason and religion, both given us by the same Divine Author, can never be antagonistic, the one to the other.

We believe that as GOD forbade false worship among the Jews, while, for special reasons, they were isolated and kept separate from the other nations of the earth, the Gentiles, so the Pope and every Christian should wish that there were in the world no errors; that we all may be "one" in faith, as the Savior prayed for us the night before he suffered. But as nations and governments are now constituted under the good providence of GOD, so does he accept them. PIUS VII crowned the first BONAPARTE, though he knew he had sworn to the constitution which gave liberty of conscience and freedom of religious worship to France. The present glorious Pontiff, like so many of his predecessors, has issued his Apostolic letters for the consecration of Bishops who swear allegiance to governments which look with equal favor, or indifference, on the various forms of Christianity, or the oppugners thereof, so long as their conduct is conformable to the civil law.

We do not believe that the Pope would allow conscience to be coerced; that he would allow an impenitent, unbelieving man to be constrained to receive Baptism or the other Sacraments; or that he believes that GOD would look without indignation on the hypocritical or the compulsory homage of the human soul. On the contrary, he acknowledges, with an ancient Father of the Church, "that it is an unheard-of procedure to "infuse faith into a man with a cudgel." He knows that there is such a thing as judicial blindness. That there are unhealthy and unsound intellects; in a word, monsters in mind as well as in body, disbelievers in deity, in morality, in religion, and even in reason; and that such, as long as they outrage not the laws of society, are to be consigned to their folly. They are better out of the Church than in it. Hence, while the Pope and every honest man regrets that the "old chaos," the anarchy of intelligences, " should be made the type of true religion," he reproves not the memorable words of the mild FENELON to king JAMES: "Grant civil toleration, not as approving as "indifferent, but as permitting with patience whatever "GOD permits, and in endeavoring to bring back men " to the truth by moral suasion."

Finally, we believe the Church was destined by JESUS CHRIST to accomplish its Divine Mission of preparing souls for heaven, under every form of government, and in every condition of human society. She condemns none where the laws are just and impartially administered. Where the laws are unjust, and rulers violate the written or the natural compact by which they claim to govern, she " interdicts not to her children patriotism." She asserts for them the inalienable right to raise both voice and hand to denounce oppression and overthrow the oppressor; but she does not encourage secret societies, she urges not to precipitate resolves, to revolution. She counsels prudence, forbearance, remonstrance, patience. She forbids individuals to involve themselves and their co-workers in irretrievable ruin by hasty, unwise, and impulsive action, which rivets chains instead of breaking them, and makes burdens heavier, and the yoke more galling, when the few attempt what only the many can accomplish.

Such do we conceive to be the teaching of the late Encyclical. Such the voice that calms the waves and stills the tempest of human passions; and such the hand that steers the bark freighted with its precious cargo of immortal souls to the secure haven of supreme happiness, for which this earthly state, no matter how arranged, is but the preparation.

J. B. PURCELL,
Archbishop of Cincinnati.

REPLY OF REV. THOMAS VICKERS TO ARCHBISHOP PURCELL.

(Published in the Cinciunati *Gazette*, November 7, 1867.)

CINCINNATI, November 5, 1867.
[The 262d Anniversary of Gunpowder Treason.]

To Archbishop Purcell, of Cincinnati:

MOST REVEREND SIR: I have waited until now before replying to your last effusion, partly because I have had something better to do, and partly because I thought it would afford you no little gratification and delight to be able to associate this reply with an anniversary which must be so full of pleasant historical remembrances to every Roman Catholic who loves free thought and "deprecates the union of church and state."

Permit me, in the first place, in your behalf, to correct a false report which some of your enemies have been circulating since the appearance of the article in the *Catholic Telegraph*, of October 30th. It has been maliciously suggested that you are incapable of producing an article couched in terms of such extraordinary courtesy, betraying such a cultivated and refined taste, coupled with such a display of logical acumen and such unexampled candor and honesty; that had you produced such a masterpiece of polemical writing, you would never have allowed it to go forth without your signature. Of course, nothing but malice and desperate ill-will could have suggested such a thing, and I joyfully take the first opportunity of freeing you from such unjust suspicions. It is perfectly evident to all careful readers that although you did not (for some reasons best known to yourself) append your signature to it, you nevertheless wrote the article; for do you not, in three several places, in referring to a former article to which your name was attached, use the first personal pronoun: "We argued," "we said," "we told him before"? and do you not say, "we republish a portion of *our* Pastoral of 1862"? Of course you wrote it; nothing but the most unscrupulous enmity could wish to deprive you of the honor which necessarily follows such eminent productions.

A SLIGHT DRAWBACK.

After this voluntary vindication of your rights, I trust you will not take it amiss if, before proceeding to examine the essential points of your reply, I make a single remark: You seem to have the slight misfortune of seeing things in documents "before you" which are not there, and of not seeing things which are there. This, unfortunately, slightly detracts from the trustworthiness of your representations, and makes the task of replying to you somewhat unpleasant. I shall have occasion to notice several cases in which this ophthalmic difficulty of yours manifests itself. First, in regard to

"FREEMEN" AND "FREE SPEECH."

You say that, "in the paper before you," I "insist" on having "inflicted no censure" on the "freemen of

Ohio" for voting against the Constitutional Amendment. In that paper I never said any such thing; on the contrary, I vindicated my right to censure them— that is, to express my opinion in regard to their action. And this right I never denied even to the Romish Church. This was not "the point, friend," as you very well know. The point was that the Romish Church claims not only the right "to tell men so," when they "think and speak what is wrong," but she claims the right to *punish* men for speaking what is contrary to her doctrines; what they say may be in itself wrong or right. This I stated just as plainly "in the paper before you" as I have done now. *Intelligibilia, non intellectum, fero.* I would suggest your delegating the controversy to some one who is not troubled with any of the various species of ophthalmia.

EMERSON.

No one respects Mr. Emerson more than I do, but I do not feel bound by his opinions, especially on matters concerning which he has but little knowledge. Now, had you searched his writings through, you could scarcely have found a paragraph with more blunders in it than the one you quoted. In the first place, no sensible, well-read man nowadays includes the fifteenth century in the Dark Ages; consequently, we do not owe the art of printing and the discovery of America to them. Furthermore, the Dark Ages neither gave us gunpowder, glass, nor chemistry; and had Mr. Emerson, at the time he wrote the paragraph in question, been at all intimately acquainted with the history of the arts and sciences, he never would have said they did. We know that glass, for instance, was used at least one thousand six hundred years before the Christian era. Why, we already find pictures of glass-blowers on Egyptian monuments. And when Mr. Emerson says that "human thought was never more active and never produced greater results in any period of the world" than in the one under discussion, the assertion is simply an historical blunder. But there is another point on which this extract from Emerson will serve you a sorry trick. Alas! you really seem doomed to perish by your own weapons. Why did not your "Guardian Angel" stay your hand before you wrote the name of

ROGER BACON?

Do you not remember that my original thesis was that the Romish Church had never tolerated free thought? Had you forgotten the cruel persecutions which this same Franciscan monk, Bacon, had to endure from the Church on account of his free thought? Had you forgotten that he was condemned *propter novitates quasdam suspectas?*—that, from 1257 until 1267, he was continually persecuted, kept most of the time in prison, and prevented from holding any intercourse with the outward world? Had you forgotten that, in 1278, when he was sixty-four years old, he was summoned to Paris, where a council of Franciscans, with the Pope's legate at their head, condemned his writings and committed him to close confinement, and that, for ten years, every effort to procure his liberation was in vain? Had you forgotten that, even after his death, the monks feared and hated his books so much that they nailed them to boards to prevent their being read, and "left them to rot amid dirt and damp?" O, most reverend sir! is this what you meant when you said that the Church only *tells* men that they are wrong when she finds them so?

FIRMILIAN.

I am not at all surprised that you seek to rid yourself of this uncomfortable adversary. His bitter opposition to the supremacy and infallibility of the Roman Bishop has always been a "thorn in the flesh" of the Romish Church. She first tried to *suppress* entirely the letter from which I quoted, and it is, therefore, not to be found in the editions of Cyprian by Erasmus and Manutius. Although it is extant in twenty-six different *codices*, it was first printed by Guil. Morellius, Paris, 1564, who was bitterly censured for his temerity by Latinus and Pamelius. But the Church, finding it impossible to suppress the letter, tried another expedient: she tried to prove it a forgery. And if it were necessary, dear sir, I could furnish you the names of quite a number of persons who tried this game besides your redoubtable friend, Marcellinus Molkenbuhr, that great critical genius (!), who also wrote a treatise to prove that the books of the New Testament were *originally written in Latin!* But even the Romish Church has long since given up the forgery-hypothesis; there is no longer any controversy on the matter. There is not a single church historian or critic, whose opinion is worth noticing, *whether Catholic or Protestant*, who does not admit the letter to be genuine. Walch, Rettberg, Lardner, Mosheim, Neander, Milner, Milman, Guericke, Gieseler, Schaaf—all admit its genuineness. Pretty good authorities, and plenty of them. But allow me to direct your attention to three Roman Catholic authorities, as these will probably weigh most with you. The first is the celebrated Tillemont, of whom Dupin said: "There is nothing which has escaped his exactness, and there is nothing obscure or intricate which his criticism has not cleared up or disentangled." If you will take the trouble to look into the *Memoires pour servir a l'Histoire Ecclesiastique* (tome 4, p. 157, et seq.), you will find that his opinion does not coincide with that of your immaculate critic. But let us come a little nearer home. If I am not mistaken, Archbishop Kenrick has, in the Catholic Church, quite a reputation for scholarship (has he not, dear sir?), and yet, in his book on the "Primacy of the Apostolic See" (5th ed., p. 116, et. seq.), he quotes the letter as genuine. The third authority is the "Church Lexicon, or Encyclopedia of Catholic Theology, edited by Heinrich Joseph Wetzer and Benedict Welte, (both Catholic professors of theology at the Catholic University of Freiburg), *aided by some of the most distinguished Catholic scholars in Germany,*" and published in twelve volumes by the well-known Catholic publisher, Herder, in Freiburg. I translate literally from vol. 4, p. 74 (published in 1850): "Cyprian consulted Firmilian, in order to learn from him more accurately the opinion and practice of the orientals in the matter in question (baptism by heretics); and Firmilian, in a long letter, not without violence, mockery, and irony, declared himself against Pope Stephen, and sought to defend the practice of the orientals. *This letter, originally written in the Greek language, was translated into Latin by Cyprian, and is found among Cyprian's Letters as epistola* 75." How could you be so in the dark, most reverend sir? I would suggest the propriety of delegating the controversy to some one better acquainted with the history of Christian literature than you seem to be.

AUGUSTINE AND AQUINAS.

In regard to these two men, I wish to ask you a few questions, which I beg you to answer *without any contortions or equivocations.* Did Augustine, knowing the laws against heresy, *call upon the civil power to enforce them against the Donatists,* or did he not? Did Thomas Aquinas *justify the punishment of heresy by death,* or did he not? Did I, or did I not, quote, in my last reply, *the exact language* of Aquinas as found not only in Migne, but *in all editions* of this author? And if I did, by what canon of ecclesiastical morals do you say I "pretend to quote" it?

THE SECULAR TRIBUNAL.

It was, of course, to be expected that you would assert that the Church had nothing to do with executing the sentence of death upon heretics—she handed them over to the secular arm (!). Now, most reverend sir, allow me to ask you another question, and to beg to this also an unequivocal answer. One instance is as good as a thousand here. Am I right in supposing that, in the year 1600, the ecclesiastical *and* the secular power *in Rome* were *both* in the hands of the Church? And if so, *what power* executed Giordano Bruno, who was *burned* there, on the 17th of February of that year, *for heresy?*

Still further, let me ask you, if the following is one

of the forty-one errors of Luther, condemned in the bull of Leo X, bearing date June 14, 1520? *"Hæreticos comburi, est contra voluntatem spiritus."* And is the following a correct translation: "To *burn* heretics is contrary to the will of the Holy Spirit"?

Furthermore, is the following a correct translation of one of the closing paragraphs of the bull of Innocent X against the errors of Jansen, dated May 31, 1653? "We likewise prescribe to *all* patriarchs, *archbishops*, bishops, etc., as well as to all inquisitors of heretical depravity, that they *utterly* restrain and repress all those who are refractory and rebellious [concerning the matter in hand] by means of the above-mentioned pains and penalties, and the other suitable remedies *juris et facti*; and, also, if it should be necessary, *by the aid of the secular arm, invoked for that purpose.*"

Furthermore, is the following a correct translation of one of the canons of the Fourth Lateran Council? "We excommunicate and condemn every heresy which exalteth its face against this holy and Catholic faith. Let such persons, when condemned, be left to the secular powers, to be punished in a fitting manner; and let the secular powers be *admonished* and, if need be, *compelled* that they should set forth an oath that, *to the utmost of their power, they will strive to* EXTERMINATE ALL HERETICS *who shall be denounced by the Church*. But if any temporal lord shall neglect to cleanse his country of this *heretical filth*, let him be bound by the chain of excommunication. If he shall scorn to make satisfaction, let it be signified to the Supreme Pontiff, that he may *declare his vassals to be absolved from their fidelity*." Did not Pope Pius V do this very thing? Did he not excommunicate Queen Elizabeth, and absolve her subjects from their oath of fealty?

How dare you, most reverend sir, falsify history by asserting that the Church had nothing to do with the "consummation" of the sentence she passed upon heretics?

PROGRESS.

I, too, thank God that "the *world* has outgrown the policy and practice" of putting men to death for an opinion. But you will permit me to doubt whether the *Church* has outgrown the principles which led her to put men to death for this cause. Allow me to call your attention to a fact which did not occur in the middle ages, to which you would seem to relegate all sympathy with killing men for opinion's sake, but in the year of grace 1862. Your brother Archbishop, Desprey, of Toulouse, published a pastoral in April, year just named, in which he called upon the faithful in his diocese to celebrate, on the 16th of May, a "glorious event, in which, three hundred years ago, the goodness of God and the succoring power of his saints had been so plainly manifested." What was this "glorious event?" *It was the butchery of four thousand Huguenots in cold blood, after they had laid down their arms and received the promise of unmolested retreat.* I think you will agree with me that the progress (?) in the Romish Church is of somewhat recent date. So long as Rome continues to manufacture saints out of the bloodiest mercenaries of the Inquisition, we may well pause and reflect. Had your visit to Rome, during the present year, most reverend sir, any thing to do with such a canonization?

THE JESUITS AGAIN.

I not only *say* "that the Jesuits' vow binds them to things contrary to the known law of God," but I can *prove* it. Do you desire me to quote still further from the "Constitutions?" I will name to you three Jesuit manuals of morals, which you undoubtedly have in your library, and beg you to look into them before proceeding further in this controversy. The first is the *Compendium Theol. Moralis,* by M. Moullet, formerly Professor in Freiburg; the second is Sættler's Commentary on the Sixth Commandment, augmented by Abbe Rousselot, Professor at the Seminary in Grenoble; the third is also a Commentary on the Sixth Commandment, with a dissertation *de matrimonio,* by Bishop Bouvier, of Mans (10th ed., Paris, 1813). How would you like to have me cite, with parallel translations, such passages as the one beginning with the following words, from the first: "*Si quis delectatur de copula cum muliere nupta,*" etc.; or this from the second: "*Expedit, prudenter et data occasione a mulieribus et etiam a puellis quærere, utrum cum bestia,*" etc.; or this from the third: "*Licet confessiones mulierum excipere, cum eis utiliter et honeste conversari, eas visitare vel decenter amplecti,*" etc.? Do, please, look into them, and let me know in your next reply whether I shall proceed.

THE PASTORAL.

There are several other points which I should like to notice, but with a word concerning your "pastoral" I will conclude. Of course, you know that the Encyclical and Syllabus were addressed to *you* as well as to all other "patriarchs, primates, *archbishops*," etc., and that *you are bound by every word of it.* But in writing your pastoral you probably remembered the instructions which Pius VII addressed to his nuntius in Vienna, in the year 1805, in which the following words occur: "We live, alas! in times of such great misfortune and such humiliation for the spouse of Christ, that *the Church is not only unable to make use of her most holy principles of deserved severity against the rebellious enemies of the faith, but* SHE DARE NOT EVEN MENTION THEM WITHOUT DETRIMENT."

May I not beg you, in conclusion, if you are still desirous of having the controversy continued, that you will delegate your side to some one who recognizes the common principles of grammar, logic, and morals?

With due respect, most reverend sir,

THOMAS VICKERS,
Minister of the First Congregational Society.

ARCHBISHOP PURCELL TO REV. THOMAS VICKERS.

(Published in the *Catholic Telegraph*, November 13, 1867.)

REV. SIR: In your lucubration, published in the Cincinnati *Gazette*, of the 7th inst., you intimate a wish to have my side of this controversy delegated to some one who recognizes the common principles of grammar, logic, and morals. Permit me, therefore, to inquire how much a quarter you will ask for teaching one as dull as I am grammar? I shall not, however, hire you as a competent pedagogue to teach me logic or morals, for you know, dear Mr. Vickers, *nemo dat quod non habet*. You have set me the example of larding your letters with Latin, and you can not find it amiss that I follow it grammatically. And, furthermore, I give you full credit for the statement of a "false report" which, you say, "some of my enemies had been circulating since the appearance of my article in the *Telegraph*, of the 30th October." Of course you heard it, or you never would have said you had. There must be a basis of truth for a flourish of rhetoric. And you wrote your last on the 5th November for the reasons given. These reasons were, doubtless, very satisfactory to your own refined mind and feelings. But you will excuse me for so much freethinking and speaking as to hint that, on that memorable occasion of the so-called "gunpowder plot," you would have taken a prominent part as Cecil's spy and Tresham's accomplice, if not Catesby's murderer, if you did not hold the dark lantern for Guy Fawkes, or import the thirty barrels of powder from Holland, or cart them from Lambeth, or cover them with old iron and firewood in the cellar of the Parliament house, and been inspired, like King James, "by the Holy Ghost," to call this mad enterprise of nine deluded fanatics a Popish plot. You see, my dear, amiable Mr. Vickers, I would rather think this of you than call you a scavenger that rakes up the kennels of history to fling dirt at the Catholics. It might be that some enemy, judging from the hot haste with which you fled from a discussion on free thought to the easier declamation about persecution, would suggest that this was for you a more congenial occupation. But I would not believe them, would you? Whatever your motives were, I thank you sincerely, cordially for the character you give Martin Luther in your sermon in Hopkins' Hall, on the 4th November. It was exceedingly kind on your part, if not a judicial blindness, to tell the truth so plainly about the "Father of the Reformation." I am delighted at the opportunity thus given, to call the attention of my beloved Catholic flock and of all sincere non-Catholic inquirers for truth to this matrix and womb of your new religion, of whom you say in your eloquent effusion: "Honor and praise be unto his name to-day, and the love of men be his unto the latest generation." Here it is: "At one time he, Martin Luther, rails at reason as a harlot, who, wholly given over to vanity, takes the soul captive with her deadly wiles. At another, he treats the Bible in a manner wholly arbitrary, rejects or retains the individual books only as they happen to coincide with, or contradict his own opinion; he calls one an epistle of straw; says of another, that it contains a number of most excellent bits of fun; and of a third, that it has neither boots nor spurs, but rides in its socks, just as he himself did when he was in the monastery." After thus practically despoiling man of the only faculty by which he holds the scepter of this world, or communes with the next before receiving the gift of revelation, the Arch-reformer robs him of free will, which he makes and calls a slave—"slave-will." The human will he makes a brute-beast—a horse—"if God rides it, it goes to God; if the devil, it goes to the devil." This makes man a mere machine. It deprives him of manhood. It takes from him all the responsibility of crime, all the merit of virtue. And Luther did not recoil from the consequences of his innovation. "Sin boldly," he exclaimed, "sin deeply; the more you sin the more you honor faith, the dearer child you are of God." And this, among others, was the advice he gave to his melancholy friend John Weller. "*Drink*," says the old debauchee to him, "drink and amuse yourself with Kate." Glory, honor, and praise be to the German Catholics of this day, and the love of man be theirs to the latest generation, who adhere to the religion of their fatherland, refusing to identify themselves with the spawn of such a reformation as he engendered. What think you, Rev. sir, of this portion of my answer? Do you see yourself in this "mirror?" Does it fairly reflect your features—your grammar, your logic, and your morals? You say "the old religion used the Church, the new one used the Bible, for—a "*crutch.*" This admission plainly shows that the "Reformation" was a principle, a process, that not one of the great reformers had any real historical and critical knowledge of the Bible—therefore, "reason and conscience" were taken captive by the Bible, and all the movements and relations of life were fettered to its letter." Think of this, young men, and old men, Christian and Evangelical associations of Cincinnati, and break your crutch, and put this old mutilated Bible—mutilated by Martin Luther and Rev. Mr. Vickers—in the alembic of conscience and reason, and take for your mental pabulum the residuum.

What will be this residuum? If you are not expert enough chemists to discover it yourselves, ask Mr. Vickers and his aids to please take you into their laboratory, you will soon learn that Christ, whom you make the head of your religion, "is a theological fiction;" that the Holy Spirit is not any more than Christ, very God, but a theological fiction; that the devil is a theological fiction—but, for your lives, do not suggest to the professor that when the devil gets a grip of him—as he surely will, "except he do penance"—it will be no fiction. If you told him this it might disturb the nice analysis. You will learn, of course, as a corollary, that hell, like Satan, is but an oriental metaphor; and that when the Gospel says Christ cast seven devils out of the sinful woman, he only cast seven oriental metaphors out of her; that when Jehovah forbids coveting, he is not to be obeyed, for he forbids free thought; and that in Deuteronomy xvii: 10, 11, 12, where he commands a man not to follow the dictates of his conscience or reason, but simply to obey the judgment of the priest, and that in penalty of disobedience and freethinking, "he shall die the death," he is more of a despot than any freeman in Ohio, New York, or Pennsylvania.

With this intelligence of the Bible, go, gentlemen of the Bible Society, and circulate these emasculated, mutilated, misinterpreted Scriptures, no longer the word of God, but Mr. Vickers'; or, if you will be honester still, tell your beneficiaries, the Bible is but a crutch, and the sooner they break it, in the name of conscience and reason, the better. And now, my dear Mr. Vickers, who make of the Bible what you make of the Reformation, a "*principle*," a "*process*," from which you evolve all the startling impieties I have enumerated, "even to the denying of our only Sovereign and Lord, Jesus Christ," do you not see that you are of those "certain men," of whom St. Jude speaks, verse 4, "who were of old marked out for this judgment" (condemnation)? Is it not the rejection of all the vital truths of Christianity in which— as Catholic writers like Bossuet have so often predicted—freethinking on religious matters drives its votaries from one error to another, until they find no resting-place but in the abyss of atheism? If you see not this, you see not what the Bible, the best of books, the book by excellence, sets before you. If you see it not, I counsel thee, with that blessed book, "to buy eye-salve" (Rev. iii: 13), to cure *thy* foul ophthalmia.

Well, you quarrel with Emerson. It is a family jar; I leave you to settle it as best you may.

But Roger Bacon! Why, sir, when you laud him, and laud Luther, you forget that it was in the bosom of our benighted Church they acquired, the one all his science, the other all his learning. The one was a Franciscan, the other an Augustinian friar, priest. Bacon, over whom you shed such crocodile tears, was called by our Church, and by his brethren, "Doctor admirabilis," the admirable Doctor, for his extraordinary knowledge of astronomy, chemistry, and mathematics. If his religious superior forbade him to lose his own precious time and turn the heads of his brother monks by writing and talking of alchemy, the philosopher's stone, judicial astrology, divining wands, and the making of a brazen head that would answer the questions proposed to it, this restraint did no serious injury to Bacon or to science.

You make a wonderful fuss about Firmilian. Why, sir, can you have so soon forgotten what I said of him so recently, that if he had used such coarse language in addressing the Pope, he only illustrated the more clearly the freethinking and speaking allowed or exercised in the Catholic Church? And if I gave his memory the benefit of a serious doubt as to the authenticity of the letter, the very array of names you quote to prove it genuine, goes only to show that many others regarded it as the spurious production of an African Donatist. And now, with all my respect for the celebrated Tillemont, and the little respect I have for many things said by his eulogist, Dupin, allow me to tell you that even Tillemont occasionally—like the "bonus Homerus"—napped. It would lead me off the road to quote for this remark the learned Alban Butler. But if Firmilian said all that is imputed to him, and more, it was on the well-known occasion of the controversy about the validity of baptism, conferred by heretics, in which St. Cyprian was mistaken and the Pope was not. Then Firmilian should have spoken as an excited partisan, forgetting that his principal—that is, St. Cyprian—called "the chair of Peter the principal church, the origin of the sacerdotal unity, whither perfidy can not find access." (Ep. 59 *ad Cornelium*, No. 10, p. 265.) As Butler says, "The warmth Cyprian betrayed in this controversy he much repented of, as appears by the book he afterward wrote on Patience." Let us hope that if Firmilian erred, like Cyprian for a time, like Cyprian he repented. But be this as it may, his opinion has not a feather's weight in the question of the Pope's supremacy. You ask me questions about Augustine, Aquinas, and yourself. Before answering—and I shall answer most categorically—allow me to congratulate you on getting into such good company. Firstly, then, St. Augustine, when reproached by the Donatists with the persecuting laws enforced against them, replied: "If any severity inconsistent with Christian lenity has, at any time, been exercised against you, it displeases all true Christians." · "No good man in the Catholic Church approves of the capital punishment of a heretic. (Lib. Contra Ep. Parmen, Ch. XIII. Contra Crescon. lib. III, Ch. 4, No. 55.)

When the Circumcellions, by acts of violence and bloodshed, had provoked the severity of the magistrate, he remonstrated with the Proconsul in Africa, beseeching him, through Jesus Christ, not to punish them capitally: "We wish not their death but their correction." (Ep. C. olim C. XXVII.)

Secondly, Aquinas: I have already quoted his declaration, which is the same as Augustine's—that the

Church's province is mercy. If they both left the vindication of human laws to the secular tribunal, it is no more than every honest man and citizen would do to-day if heretics made war upon society. You remember how near we were once to a conflict with the Mormons for threatened resistance to the laws of the land, and why the people of Nauvoo expelled them from their borders.

Thirdly, I answer yourself by saying that you grossly wronged St. Augustine when you made him the author of persecution for heresy whom others have followed. With the Bible and the civil law they regarded as criminals the false prophets and the false teachers who brought in *sects of perdition,* "denying the Lord who bought them," (St. Peter, 2d. Ep. Ch. II. V. 1,) and who sought to enforce their sectarianism and lawlessness by the sword. The third and fourth councils of Lateran were mixed assemblies of the spiritual and temporal powers. While the Church approves of the enactments passed " against offenders by whom every regard for decorum was removed, the marriage tie dissolved, and divine and human laws subverted," (vid: Ep. Sti. Leo. ad Turibium): yet the Council (4th Sec.) expressly forbids clergymen to sign their names to any document connected with capital punishment. I need not here remind you that Catholics in these United States have not been the authors, but the victims, of intolerance and oppression. The faggots, fire, and flames which you read of, where they were not named in the text of Aquinas, were used unmercifully against us, as they had been against the unoffending Quakers, in Charlestown, Mass., Philadelphia, and other places, even from the days of our colonial bondage to Great Britain. And the House of Refuge, where no priest is allowed to speak to scores of Catholic children, some of them immured for years for trivial offenses; and the public schools, for whose erection and endowment we Catholics are taxed so pitilessly, should shame you and every bigoted auxiliary and ungenerous foe to silence and penance. You see, sir, that *our world "has not outgrown the practice."*

I shall not follow you, sir, where you seem so anxious to lead—into the discussion of immoralities so falsely attributed to the writings of Catholic societies or theologians. The pretended monk, Leahy, who edified the cities and some of the Protestant pulpits of the United States with such obscene caricatures, may serve you for a model and exemplar. You know he finished his career by committing murder, and a sentence for life to the Wisconsin Penitentiary—from which the wretch was reprieved, if we are informed aright, at the prayer of one of the worthiest of Catholic prelates, Right Rev. Bishop Henni, of Milwaukee. After his release he begged permission to go through the country refuting his own calumnies, but we spurned him, knowing that they "who touch pitch will be defiled by it;" so do I scorn to follow you in his wake. You who rob the world of its God and Redeemer, you who nickname the Bible *a crutch;* what have you ever done for society or religion? Where are your hospitals, your orphan asylums; your refuges for penitents, for any of all the various forms of human misery? What wounds have you healed, what tears have you dried, what sorrows have you soothed, what death-beds have you sanctified, you who make Christ a "theological fiction," and the Bible "a crutch," to be cast away? The reason and the conscience which you vainly, not to say wickedly, seek to substitute for both, will sadly fail you, as they do humanity in the hour of peril and of sorest need. They have lured their followers in all ages into pits and ditches. Reason, which man's iniquity soon perverted, taught him to worship his passions for gods, and conscience was its accomplice.

Bruno, whom you should have called by his Italian name of Giordano Bruni, was, after he had doffed the Dominican habit and apostatized, driven from Geneva by Calvin and Beza, with whom you must first settle the account of his persecution. He denied, like you, the most important truths of religion; those held by Jews and Christians having been classed by him with the fables of pagans and idolaters. "Reason and conscience" he made, like you, the only arbiters of vice and virtue— and this as he understood them. The extravagance of his imagination equaled that of his logic. From Wittemburg, where he turned Lutheran, he was also banished for his assaults on all who dared oppose his irreligious follies. He then returned to his native country, and continuing to dogmatize and abuse the Pope, as the "beast," he met the fate he merited, for the Pope was temporal as well as spiritual ruler, and bound by his duty to preserve the States of the Church from the fury of the fanatic. In this the Pope did nothing but what Pio Nono would have had a right to do had Garibaldi been captured by his little army in the late invasion of Rome. Had the infidel Buccaneer of both hemispheres succeeded, he would have, like an hyena, broken into the tombs of the holy apostles and scattered their sacred ashes to the winds; he would have plundered churches and profaned the tabernacles of the Holy Eucharist, and filled the Eternal City with ruins. Under such circumstances, I say openly, and you may make whatever use you please of the admission, the death of the miscreant would have been a duty and a benefit.

I am, sir, in the true faith and love of Christ, whom you are every day blaspheming,   Yours,

J. B. PURCELL,
Archbishop of Cincinnati.

REJOINDER BY REV. THOMAS VICKERS.

(Published in the Cincinnati *Gazette*, November 22, 1867.)

To the Editor of the Cincinnati Gazette:

If the honest and intelligent readers of the *Gazette*, have attentively read the last letter, which Archbishop Purcell has seen fit to address to me, there is little occasion to burden your columns with a reply. At any rate, a brief survey of some of the peculiarities of the controversy will suffice.

I may say, in passing, that inasmuch as the greater part of my last letter was taken up with the treatment of Popes, Councils, so-called Fathers, and great dignataries of the Romish Church, it would seem, to say the least, to be somewhat indecorous, and to betray a want of *self*-respect, when the Archbishop accuses me of "raking up the KENNELS OF HISTORY." Still, I have no objection—*suum cuique!*

THE ARCHBISHOP'S METHOD OF DISCUSSION.

At the close of my letter of November 5th, I requested the Archbishop, if he wished to continue the controversy, to delegate his side to some one who recognized the common principles of grammar, logic, and morals. It is now in place to develop more clearly why I did this, and why I was compelled to do it. There is not, I am sure, in the whole literature of the old scholastic wrangles, a parallel to the controversial method of the Archbishop. An instance or two will suffice to exhibit this method in all its archiepiscopal brilliancy.

In my sermon of October 14th, I had referred to certain passages in the "Summa" of Thomas Aquinas, as showing that Aquinas justified the burning of heretics, and I had indicated the exact places where these passages were to be found. Thereupon Archbishop Purcell had the audacity to deny that any such passages occurred in the places indicated, meekly offering to exhibit his copy of the Summa to any one who might visit him, but taking good care not to print the words of Aquinas. In reply I recited the exact words in the original, taking them from the exact places originally assigned. In my sermon I had not pretended to cite the precise words; I had spoken of the "burning" of heretics, because I knew that the horrible meaning of the pious ecclesiastical brocard: "*ecclesia non sitit sanguinem* (the Church does not thirst after blood)" found its exposition in the "merciful" substitution of the torch for the sword. I knew how Huss, and Bruno, and Savonarola, and the myriad victims of the Inquisition had perished. I knew that the record of the "merciful disposition of the Church," of which the Archbishop speaks again and again, was written, not in blood, but *in flames*. Now, the precise words of Aquinas, as I afterward cited them literally, were, that heretics were to be *killed* ("*occidi*"), or, in another passage, *exterminated from the world* ("*a mundo exterminari*"), or, in still another passage, *not to be liberated from the sentence of death* ("*non tamen ut liberentur a sententia mortis*"). It would seem that these words were sufficiently explicit; although Aquinas did not specify the method by which heretics were to be exterminated, the method of the Church was *burning*. And these words were conclusive against the Archbishop, for he himself had adduced Aquinas as one of the illustrious many who attested the freedom of thought in the Catholic Church. Now, what did the Archbishop say or do after this? He did not dare directly to deny the genuineness of the passages I had quoted; but he dared to write a pretended editorial, from which he omitted his signature, and to *insinuate* that the words I had cited were not genuine, by mentioning them as words which I "pretended to quote."

He, furthermore, resorted to the subterfuge of claiming that the Church had nothing to do with the extermination of heretics, because she simply handed them over for punishment to the temporal power! To this it would have been a sufficient answer, that whenever this "handing over" took place the Church had complete control of the temporal power; but waiving this, I called the attention of the Archbishop to the case of Giordano Bruno, who was burned at Rome, where both the temporal and ecclesiastical powers were in the hands of the Pope. And now, mark the triumphant rejoinder of the Archbishop in his last letter. He admits that the Pope, who was "temporal as well as spiritual ruler," burned Bruno; but he says that the name of the victim was Giordano Bruni, and not Bruno; that Bruno or Bruni "apostatized;" that he was "driven from Geneva by Calvin and Beza;" that he was "banished from Wittenberg (where he turned Lutheran) for his assaults on all who dared oppose his irreligious follies;" that he "returned to his native country, and continuing *to dogmatize and abuse the Pope*," he "*met the fate he merited.*" But the Archbishop does not stop here. He says, with unexampled candor, that it would have been the "duty" of Pio Nono to treat Garibaldi, if he had caught him, in just the same manner!!!

I need make no comments on this brazen and bloodthirsty utterance. The public now knows the real sentiments of the Archbishop, and will judge him accordingly. But the Archbishop's zeal again betrays his limping scholarship.

The simple fact is, that Bruno was not "driven from Geneva by Calvin and Beza;" that he never "became a Lutheran;" and that he never was "banished from Wittenberg;" therefore I have no need to "first settle the account of his persecution" with the Protestant reformers. From what trustworthy (?) Catholic historian did the Archbishop get his information this time?

FIRMILIAN AGAIN.

Another instance of Archbishop Purcell's polemical practice. I had occasion to allude to Firmilian's letter to Cyprian. In his article of October 30th, the Archbishop pompously announced that, in citing this letter, I "floundered in the mire again," and added: "If the gentleman (Mr. Vickers) reads the dissertation in 4to, written by Marcellinus Molkenbuhr, and printed in Munster, Westphalia, in 1790, *he will find* that the letter in question *was falsely attributed to Firmilian*, and that it was, on the contrary, the production of an African Donatist of the fourth century." In reply, I showed that this man Molkenbuhr was an idiot, who had, among others, written a treatise to prove that the books of the New Testament were originally composed in Latin, and not in Greek, and that the most eminent Catholic divines of our day, including Archbishop Kenrick, recognized the genuineness of Firmilian's letter. All this does not disconcert the Archbishop in the least; although he had a moment before *not simply doubted* the genuineness of the letter, but pronounced it spurious, and accused me of "floundering in the mire," because I did not know that it was spurious, he has now the ecclesiastical candor to write: "If I give his (Firmilian's) memory the benefit of a serious doubt as to the authenticity of the letter, the very array of names you quote to prove it genuine goes only to show *that many others regarded it as the spurious production of an African Donatist.*" What a brilliant specimen of archiepiscopal logic!

EMERSON AGAIN.

Another fine specimen of archiepiscopal dialectics. The Archbishop has the misfortune to quote Emerson to prove that the so-called "Dark Ages" were "ages of light," but when I show him that Emerson did not understand what he was talking about, he turns round and exclaims, with the most charming nonchalance: "Well, it is a family jar [between you and Mr. Emerson]. I leave you to settle it as best you may" (!)

QUESTION AND ANSWER.

Nothing, however, is so characteristic of the conduct of the Archbishop, during this controversy, as the manner in which he has asked and answered questions.

There are, in general, two sorts of weapons on which he has wholly relied, and which he has used alternately as convenience suited. On the one hand, he thought to annihilate me by throwing high-sounding names, the titles of ponderous folios, and old cathedrals at me; and on the other, he cunningly and (I might say) impudently sought to make me commit myself on points of Christian doctrine, wholly irrelevant to the discussion, so as to damage me in the estimation of orthodox Protestants, and thus destroy the influence of any facts or arguments I might bring against him. Now, although I did not for a moment recognize *his right* to catechise me on matters of doctrine, I, nevertheless, answered his questions *simply and directly;* and, by allowing my sermon on the "Rise and Progress of Protestantism," to be printed gratuitously, gave him material for the greater part of his last coarse diatribe, which is mainly devoted to inflaming the prejudices of Protestants against me.

But what does the Archbishop do when I ask him to answer questions *pertinent to the discussion?* He, with a single exception, already noticed, either pretends to answer them "most categorically," but does not come within a thousand miles of them, or he proceeds as if they had never been asked. In my last letter, for instance, I asked him some very pointed questions, which required a direct answer in the affirmative or negative. It will be interesting to look at them again, and at the treatment they receive.

QUESTIONS.	ANSWERS.
1. "Did Augustine, knowing the laws against heresy, *call upon the civil power to enforce*	1. Two passages quoted from Augustine to show that he did not approve of punishing here-

them against the Donatists, or did he not?"

2. "Did Thomas Aquinas *justify the punishment of heresy by death,* or did he not?"

3. "Did I, or did I not, quote, in my last reply, *the exact language of* AQUINAS, as found not only in Migne, but *in all editions* of this author? and if I did, by what canon of ecclesiastical morals do you say I 'pretended to quote' it?"

4. "Is the following one of the forty-one heresies of Luther, condemned by the bull of Leo X, bearing date of June 14th, 1520? 'To BURN (*comburi*) heretics is contrary to the will of the Holy Spirit.'"

5. "Did Innocent X, in his bull against the heresies of Jansen (May 31, 1653), direct all *archbishops,* etc., to *utterly restrain and repress,* by means of pains and penalties, all adherents of Jansen, and *to call in the aid of the secular arm,* if necessary, to that end?"

6. "Did the Fourth Lateran Council decree that the secular powers be *admonished,* and, if need be, COMPELLED, to take an oath that, *to the utmost of their power,* they will strive to EXTERMINATE ALL HERETICS DENOUNCED BY THE CHURCH?"

tics with death, or with a "severity inconsistent with Christian lenity" (whatever that may mean). Not answered at all.

2. The repetition of a quotation, *dishonestly* torn from its context, as I have previously shown. No answer.

3. "You grossly wronged AUGUSTINE (!) when you made him the author of persecution for heresy." (*Ego de caseo loquor, tu de creta respondes.* And, by the way, what I said of Augustine was not that he was "the author of persecution for heresy," but that he was "the first man in the occident *to elaborate a theory* for compulsion in religious matters for the persecution of heretics.")

4. No answer.

5. *Altum silentium.*

6. "The Fourth Council of Lateran was a mixed assembly of the spiritual and temporal powers" (!).

(Another dishonest subterfuge. The Archbishop knows that, under Innocent III, the secular princes were but the slaves of the Church; that In-

7. "Finally, to cap the climax, I asked the Archbishop whether his recent visit to Rome had any thing to do with elevating a certain bloody inquisitor to *saintship* in the Roman Catholic Church?"	nocent, by whose authority the Council was assembled, and who controlled all its actions, claimed to be the *temporal* ruler of the whole earth. *Romanus Pontifex non puri hominis, sed veri Dei vicem gerit in terris.* Inn. Lib. I, ep. 335. *Dominus Petro non solum universam Ecclesiam, sed totum reliquit sæculum gubernandum.* Inn. Lib. II, ep. 209. The Archbishop furthermore knows that the Council of Trent was also a "mixed assembly," and that its canons and decrees are none the less binding on him on that account. 7. *Altissimum silentium.*

HERESY AND PERSECUTION.

But the Archbishop accuses me of "fleeing (?) in hot haste from a discussion on free thought to the easier declamation about persecution." Was the Archbishop, like his "*bonus Homerus*," asleep when he wrote this? or did he suppose that it made no difference whether he wrote sense or nonsense, so long as the name of an Archbishop was appended to it? Free thought and persecution! Is not this just what we have been talking about all the time? Did I not, in the very first address, assert that, "wherever free thought attempted to show itself, the Church immediately crushed it out?" Was not this persecution with a vengeance? And was it not this very assertion at which the Archbishop took such great offense? What need, then, of "fleeing"?

But if any one has "fled," it is the Archbishop himself. He has fled from the most notorious facts of history, and it is impossible to get him to face them. He has sought, by every artifice, to maintain the most untenable of all possible propositions—that the Romish Church allows liberty of conscience, and never persecutes for opinion's sake. I purpose examining one or two more witnesses on this point before leaving the matter. The first is Cardinal Bellarmin (1542–1621). What does he say? In the twenty-first chapter of the third book of his work, entitled *"De Laicis,"* he teaches and proves at length "that heretics, condemned by the Church, may be punished with temporal punishment, and *even with death*" (*posse hæreticos ab Ecclesia damnatos temporalibus pœnis, etiam morte mulctari*).. In the following chapter (the twenty-second), he answers various objections; among others, the one that the Church had never burnt heretics, and says that such an objection could only arise from ignorance or willful misstatement; "for that heretics were *often burned* by the Church may be proved by adducing a few from many examples" (*nam quod hæretici sint sæpa ab Ecclesia combusti, ostendi potest, si adducamus pauca exempla de multis*). Another objection is, that experience shows that terror is not useful. Bellarmin replies: "Experience proves the contrary; for the Donatists, Manichaens, and Albigenses were routed and annihilated by arms" (*experientia est contrarium: nam Donatistæ, Manichæi, et Albigenses armis profligati et extincti sunt*). Rather explicit, is he not?

The next witness is Peter Dens (*"reverendus ac eru-*

ditissimus dominus"). In his "*Theologia, ad usum seminariorum et sacrœ Theologiœ alumnorum,*" printed at Mechlin, "*superiorum permissu,*" in the edition of 1845 (vol. 2, pp. 332, 333), under the heading, "*de pœnis criminis hæresis,*" he advocates the punishment of heretics *by death,* and quotes the very passage which the Archbishop says I "pretended to quote" from Aquinas!

This book was first published in the latter half of the last century, but, in the year 1808, the Romish clergy of Dublin unanimously agreed that it was "the best work, and the safest guide in theology for the Irish clergy;" and it is still regarded as high authority.

The next witness is Pope Gregory XVI. In his encyclical letter, published in 1832, he calls *liberty of conscience* "an absurdity, a delirium," and the *freedom of the press* a thing "most foul, and never to be enough execrated and detested."

The next is the famous Cardinal Pacca, the Pope's Prime Minister. In the same year (1832) he wrote: "If, in certain circumstances, *prudence compels us to tolerate them* [*i. e.,* the liberty of worship and the liberty of the press], as one tolerates a less evil to avoid a greater, *such doctrines can not ever be presented by a Catholic as good, or as a desirable thing.*" Furthermore, one of the greatest Catholic theologians of the present day (Perrone, I, 265) says: "Religious toleration is *impious and absurd,*" and he goes to great trouble to prove it so.

But the animus of the Romish Church is best shown by what she, at this moment (according to the *Pontificalia Romana, de Consecratione Episcoporum,* Mechliniæ, 1855, vol. I, p. 84, seq.), requires of every bishop in the ceremony of his consecration. Among other questions, the bishop elect is asked, "Dost thou curse, also, every heresy raising itself against this Holy Catholic Church?" He answers, "I do curse it." This is ratified by the oath of consecration. Having sworn to defend, against every one, the Roman Papacy and the *royalties* of St. Peter, and to observe, and cause to be observed by others, the rules of the sacred fathers, the apostolic decrees, ordinances or disposals, reservations, provisions, and commands," he adds: "*Heretics, schismatics, and rebels against our Lord* (the Pope), *or his successors, I will, to the utmost of my power,* PERSECUTE AND ASSAIL." (*Hæreticos, schismaticos, et rebelles eidem domino nostro vel successoribus prædictis* PRO POSSE PERSEQUAR ET OPPUGNABO.)

Now what, in the face of all the facts I have cited, does it amount to when the Archbishop raves about Circumcellions, false prophets, false teachers, persecuted Quakers, colonial bondage to Great Britain, house of refuge, apostate monks, etc.? "*Quid enim est tam furiosum quam verborum sonitus inanis, nullâ subjectâ sententiâ?*"

THE MONK LEAHY.

Before concluding, it may be well to notice one thing more. The name of one of the apostate monks, one Leahy, is flung at me by the Archbishop in his last letter. It is the only new name, I believe, which he has vouchsafed, this time, to bring into the controversy. This man Leahy, the Archbishop says, committed murder. I trust that I am not to be held answerable for the crimes of all the apostate monks, for I am not one of them. Of Leahy, especially, I know nothing—probably because I was in Germany when his crime was committed. But had the Archbishop forgotten, when he cited this apostate monk, what he had said, a moment before, in the same letter, about other monks? Had he forgotten that he apostrophized me in the words: "Why, sir, when you laud him (Roger Bacon) and laud Luther, you forget that it was in the bosom of our benighted Church they acquired—the one all his science, the other all his learning? The one was a Franciscan, the other an Augustinian friar—priest." Now, if the Archbishop thus insists that the Church deserves all the credit of Bacon's science and Luther's learning, *must he not, pari ratione, vindicate to his Church all the credit for Leahy's murder?*

But enough, and more than enough. In conclusion, I will only glance at

WHAT THE CONTROVERSY HAS SETTLED.

Yes, there are some things which this controversy has already definitely settled. Not only a recognition of the common principles of grammar, logic, and morals, is necessary to the participants in such a controversy as this, but also a thorough acquaintance with the subject in all its branches and bearings, and, last, but not least, *the ability to keep one's temper*. Now I do not hesitate to say, that no fair-minded, intelligent person, who has followed the course of the controversy, can help seeing that Archbishop Purcell has been grievously at fault in *all* these respects. He has hitherto had at least the *reputation* of scholarship—nay, I understand he has been regarded as almost infallible in this direction; he has hitherto had the reputation of being mild and humane in feeling, polished and courteous in manner;

these were illusions, which he has done his best to dispel. I trust he is satisfied with the result. Of one thing I am sure—his "warfare is accomplished;" he will have no more controversies—at least, not of this sort—for no one will have sufficient respect for his opinion, or sufficient confidence in his honesty of purpose, to run the risk of being a mark for his coarse and brutal invective.

As for me, I can only say, that neither the foaming anathemas of Archbishop Purcell, nor the letters threatening personal violence, which some of his "beloved Catholic flock" have troubled themselves to write me, will prevent me from denouncing bigotry, intolerance, and mendacity whenever and wherever it seems to be my duty.

THOMAS VICKERS,
Minister of the First Congregational Society.

ARCHBISHOP PURCELL'S REPLY.

(Published in the *Catholic Telegraph*, December 4, 1867.)

TEXT.—"Their God is a fiction, their Bible a crutch."

REV. MR. VICKERS, in the Cincinnati *Gazette*, of November 22d, plays Punchinello in the Italian puppet show. When his antagonist had left him floored on the stage, Punchinello, finding himself alone, jumps up with a swagger and cries out "Victory."

In his conceited self-glorification he forgets all the ignorance and inconsistency he had manifested, and false statements he had made in his encounter with me, and winds up with a statement of what the controversy has settled.

I shall follow his example, and as the Cincinnati *Gazette* did not publish my last two letters, I shall disturb his false security by giving those who seek the truth an opportunity, through the columns of the *Catholic Telegraph*, to "hear the other side," or apply the rule, as a Latin scholar might prefer, of "*audi alteram partem.*"

1st. Mr. Vickers, in his speech at the laying of the corner-stone of the German Lutheran Church of St. John, in this city, professed to have been chosen to express the sympathy of the American population with the occasion. This, we assert, was, to begin with, a false statement. By whom was he chosen? At what convention? Did the Episcopalians, the Presbyterians, the Baptists, the Methodists, the Catholics—no inconsiderable portion of the American population of Cincinnati—choose him? What vouchers, what credentials but his own unreliable word did he exhibit? What delegates then on hand to indorse his statement? *"Silentium."*

2d. He spat upon the corner-stone, and insulted all the denominations I have named by saying, "brutally," to use one of his own expressions, "That the Church, whether Roman Catholic or Protestant, holds free thought and free investigation as heretical as ever; that she is forsaken of all thinkers; she is the object of mockery and contempt, and has become a prey to the rats and mice of history." This, it must be acknowledged, is modest and consistent on the part of the chosen representative of the American population of Cincinnati, and quite complimentary to the chosen of all denominations.

3d. His ignorance. In his sermon in Hopkins' Hall, reported in the city papers, of October 14th, he says: "The new dogma of the Immaculate Conception makes Jesus the cause of his own grandmother's having brought his mother into the world without due process of nature." I ask the reader not to overlook his attempt to escape from the humiliation to which this betrayal of his inexcusable ignorance justly subjected the pastor of Hopkins' Hall First Congregational Society.

4th. He illustrated his appreciation of every man's right to "free thought" by launching the anathema of despotism, or nicknaming and reviling as despots all who voted at the last elections, that is to say, hundreds of thousands, contrary to his dictation. This audacity shows that it is only owing to the circumstances of a change of time and place that Mr. Vickers is not a Torquemada.

5th. The gentleman denies that free thought was ever tolerated in the Catholic Church. And when I asked him when and where there appeared on this earth better or deeper thinkers or writers than the fathers of the early ages—Tertullian, Cyprian, Augustine, Lactantius, etc.; or their successors, Aquinas, Venerable Bede, and hundreds of others, whom it were tedious to mention, in the long lapse of ages which he calls dark—he quarrels with Emerson, of his own school of irreligion, and, of course, with the Protestant Carlyle for eulogizing the activity of the human mind and the light and the science, and the materials of mental advancement and knowledge accumulated at that period, saying that "Emerson did not know what he was talking about." But when the glorious works of the fathers and doctors of the Church rise up as monuments to vindicate the fact that they thought freely, investigated thoroughly, spoke and wrote fearlessly, he eludes the force of this argument by saying that they advocated punishment of heresy. To this objection we made many answers: first, it does not disprove the fact of their having thought freely if they thought wrong; secondly, they had the teaching and example of the God of the Old Testament, whom Mr. Vickers probably has not yet disowned, for their opposition to false religion; thirdly, they had learned from the New Testament that heresy was classed by the inspired writers with the most grievous crimes; fourthly, they were aware of all that true believers had to suffer from Pagans, Circumcellions, Donatists, Arians, Albigenses, Moors; and, in later years, the Hussites, the Peasants, Ziska, and the "endless army of warriors for the light and truth of God," who, as Mr. Vickers acknowledges, "requited with bloody vengeance what their brothers had suffered." Fifthly, if the Church had to define what constituted heresy, that Christians may avoid it, it was the civil authorities, as guardians of public security, that inflicted the penalties incurred by outrages on society. As proof of this we refer him to the able letters of the Count de Maistre, which we have no time to do more than name. Sixthly, the Protestant churches of England and Scotland on either side of the Atlantic, in later centuries and years, have sins enough to answer for on this charge. Finally, Mr. Vickers, and all who think with him, having had, like us, Catholic ancestors, are bound as much as we are to apologize for their conduct, if apology it needs. We are no advocates of coercion. God and the Church allow men to think. Man, if he think not, is man no more. But God and the Church forbid man to think evil. Here is the distinction which Mr. Vickers has not the sagacity to see or the candor to acknowledge. God, in the seventeenth chapter of Deuteronomy, in the Decalogue, and in the New Testament, forbids him to prefer his own judgment to that of the authority which he has commissioned to teach him, forbids him to covet, and if he do, he reserves the right to punish him. So the Church can not, any more than God, prevent man from thinking, but she warns him that the "Searcher of hearts" knows when he willfully thinks evil, as Cain did, and for this shall "sin be at the door."

6th. I reiterate, there is no power, human or divine, that forces a man to believe a religion or any thing else against his own honest and enlightened convictions; and, at the same time, I maintain, with the Pope, it is a damnable error to teach that paganism or idolatry is true; that Mormonism or Mohammedanism is true; that Christ is a fiction, hell a fiction, or the Bible a crutch, even when man's perverted reason leads him to such ridiculous and false conclusions.

7th. I hold that it is an error to maintain that the Church *ought* to be separated from the State, and the State from the Church, for these should act in harmony, like soul and body; and God declares that kings should be the nursing fathers and queens the nurses of his Church or people. (Is. xlix: 23.) But, in truth, the Church needeth no such nursing. It succeeded during the first three centuries not only without the aid of kings, but in spite of their hostility; it survived the ten bloody persecutions of the "Beast" of paganism with its ten horns; it suffered cruelly from the Arian kings, from the Henrys, the Barbarossas; it has suffered awfully in the suppression of its religious orders, the confiscation of its property, the incarceration and death of its ministers in Spain, in Portugal, in England, in Italy, in South American provinces, in Mexico, in France. It is even now suffering in every one of those countries, showing what the union of the Church and State—not as the State *ought* to be, but as it is—does for her. And when it pretended to act in concert with her, its friendship was often worse to her than its enmity; it made her responsible for its misdeeds, it stifled her in its embrace. I, therefore, want no such union. I deprecate it.

CHURCH AND STATE.

No one, at the present day, is permitted, by free-thinkers, to hint that a union of Church and State is desirable. It is an exploded notion, one of the antique memories, baneful and distressing. All the liberals, the pioneers of sensational maxims in politics, the transcendental boobies from German universities, the conservative Catholics, and the fools who run loose through society, all forbid the union between the State and the Church. The question is as near an unanimous negative as it is probable any question will ever approach in the world.

This is very consoling. Here is one point at least in the position of the Church against which the reproaches of the enemy can not be directed. Here, as the saying is, she has a sure thing. She has been put out in the cold, as it is sometimes proposed to do with New England, and she has no friend inside. The State house door is locked and bolted, and she is told by the police to move on.

This is all quite proper. Ecclesiastics, we are told, are poor politicians. They do not know how to manage public affairs. They interfere with the cozy tranquillity which statesmen desire to enjoy when they labor for the public good, and are at the same time so very unselfish, so practically disinterested. Moreover, the Church is excluded because the State loves her. It distresses the politicians when they think of the impropriety of the person of the Church wearing the livery of the State. Her mission, they insist, is higher and holier. Her sacred vestments must not be soiled by the hands of demagogues. To guard her as much as possible from a profanation so dreadful, she must be excluded from all participation in human affairs. Her proper place is Olympus where she is expected to doze and occasionally nod, but she must do this gently, so as not to shake the spheres. This is all quite correct and becoming. If any wrong is committed, any tyranny practiced, the Church is relieved from any responsibility, because she can not interfere to prevent it. She is confined to a position in space where the least possible communication with mankind is permitted. She is tolerated, respected, often abused; no more.

And all this is quite proper, because the difference between the condition of the world now and at the time when she guided the course of events, is manifest proof of incapacity. She did not know how to govern, as the historians say, and do n't they know? Has it not been hammered into the heads of men for more than three hundred years, and is it not, therefore, incontrovertible that the Church is incapable?

How eminently superior is the State! When the Church ruled, in the olden time, then there were no national debts, now we have them in all their glory! When the Church ruled, taxes were scarcely known in the world, now let us be thankful and joyful, every man, from the millionaire to the pauper, knows all about them. Here is an invincible argument to exclude the Church and her ignorant ecclesiastics from political interference. Who can contemplate these facts and not acknowledge the wisdom of the change! When the Church ruled, there was no paper money; the foolish old thing insisted that gold and silver should be the basis of trade; now survey the magnificent prospect! A steam engine making money and thousands of millions circulated far and wide, and the people, like Oliver Twist, though with a greater capacity to swallow, asking for more, more, more! Here is a grand feat of statesmanship, which old Mother Church would have never thought of. When the Church ruled, her religious houses were open to the poor: there was employment for all who wanted it. It was no disgrace to be in poverty. Now, the poor are shut up in the almshouse, fed on the lowest and meanest diet, made to feel their degradation in their inmost heart, and, as in English work-houses, the husband separated from the wife and the children from both. What an immense advance is this on the miserable state of affairs which existed in the middle ages, the dark, yes, the exceedingly dark ages! There were no trades unions then, no strikes—those desperate but useless efforts of labor to escape the hand of the capitalist—which is another proof of the ignorance of those times and the unskillful legislation of the Church. All history can be produced to show the incapacity of ecclesiastics to rule the State. There were no great standing armies when she was in power; now they consist of millions of men, taken from the industry of the land, which groans to support them. The grandest country that ever invited men to her cities and fields is severed, and starvation exists where plenty should prevail, and the Church is deprived of all the honor which should result from such a state of things, because she had no hand in producing this ruin of a nation. The State knew better than the Church; it was the State that did it, to her be all the honor!

From these few samples it will be inferred that the exclusion of the Church from the councils of the State throughout all the world works beautifully for the happiness of men. It was a noble thought—and we all advocate it—which separated the two powers, but it will not be considered, we hope, presumptuous if we hint that the world with all it conveniences, trade, manufactures, and expositions, has no reason to scoff so often at the Church. The State has managed to reduce human affairs in the old and new world to the worst possible condition, and the Church is deprived of what should be her share in the honors by her exclusion from its councils. Let all the world, therefore, rejoice, that the State and the kingdom of God have no connection.

8th. I propose to circulate the whole Bible, the true Bible, the Holy Scriptures—to place a copy of these in every Catholic home. But not a mutilated Bible, not a Bible from which have been torn the books of Judith, Esther, Tobias, Baruch, Ecclesiasticus, Wisdom, three chapters of Daniel, and the Maccabees—not a mistranslated, perverted, pestilent Bible, such as the Pope has never condemned in language too severe.

And yet it is a singular inconsistency in Mr. Vickers to say a word about the Bible when he says with Luther, the Epistle of St. James—which Protestants as well as Catholics retain—is an "epistle of straw;" that another book of the sacred canon contains "bits of fun;" and all of which, straw or no straw, fun or no fun, Mr.

Vickers calls a crutch, to be cast away in the name of that reason which Luther called a "harlot." Henceforth we leave him in the hands of the orthodox ministers of Cincinnati and the Young Men's Christian and Biblical Societies. Let them look to it.

9th. The Jesuits. They need no defense of mine. They have filled the world with their scholarship, their science, their missionary labors, their saintly men—like St. Francis Xavier. Postulants, before they enter their houses, know that walking in his footsteps they can not go astray; that the order was and is approved by the Church; that the doors and windows are open for them to leave it when they please; and that during the long years they are required to remain novices or scholastics, they have to study the constitutions; and finally vow obedience only when they have been taught and convinced that superiors can not oblige them to any thing contrary to the known will of God.

10th. The gentleman, as well as certain newspapers, that is, *The Nation*, pretends to place me in opposition to the Encyclical and Syllabus, and threatens me with Pontifical displeasure. This is another instance of his lack of good faith. He knows that I said in my pastoral, of the judgment of His Holiness in the Encyclical and Syllabus, "We receive it implicitly, we bow to it reverently, we embrace it cordially, we hail it gratefully. To us it is as the voice of God on Sinai, on the Jordan, on Thabor." And we took, further, the superfluous pains to show that every error condemned in the Syllabus was, as the Pope declared it to be, "pernicious."

11th. The *hiatus* in the letter of Mr. Vickers, Cincinnati *Gazette*, 22d November, written and published when I was attending to official duties in St. Mary's, Auglaize County; in Middletown, Dayton, Urbana, can be filled satisfactorily to every candid mind with answers contained in my letter, published in the *Catholic Telegraph*, of the 13th November, concerning Firmilian, Augustine, Aquinas. There is no necessity for following the gentleman in his endless repetitions. But that he may understand how far I am from reticence or concealment, I answer as categorically, as pertinently, as closely to the question as human language can answer, that Augustine, Aquinas, popes, and cardinals did teach that the secular power was bound to repress heresy; for it was in their days, as well as since and before, connected with disturbance of the public peace, with outrages on society, with gross violation of decency and morals. Is this what he calls *altissimum silentium?* or can he deny that I answered this question, illustrating it with the case of the Mormons, more than once before?

12th. I answer that I believe the saints canonized by the immortal and saintly Pio Nono, in 1867, deserve the honor, whatever brutal names Mr. Vickers may choose to call them.

13th. Instead of having any thing to retract, I must add to what I have said of Giordano Bruno, on the faith of a most reliable historian, De Feller, in his Biographie Universelle. He had, after his apostasy, in consequence of his quarrel with Calvin and Beza, to fly from Geneva, and Paris, and Wittenburg. In this last city he turned Lutheran; and finding even this Protestant city too hot for him, on account of his turbulent spirit and his open denial of all the most important revealed truths held by Jews and Christians, he traveled through different places in Germany. He went to Rome, of course, to circulate the books which, under the patronage of the delectable Virgin Queen Elizabeth and Sir Philip Sidney, he had published in London, on the *expulsion of the triumphant beast,* and there met the fate he deserved.

14th. And this caps the climax of Mr. Vickers' ignorance, inconsistency, and lack of logic. He argues that if I claim for the Church the credit of Bacon's science and Luther's learning, I "must, *pari ratione,* for a like reason, also give her credit for Leahy's murder." Now, reasoning like this would make Christ as responsible for the treason and suicide of Judas, as he was deserving of the homage of men and angels for the teachings of the inspired Evangelists and the Apostles. Such is Mr. Vickers' ratiocination.

15th. I have thus, on my side, and in my own better right, shown "what this controversy has settled," and *I am* perfectly satisfied with the result. I have received no "threatening letters," but oral and written felicitations from both Protestants and Catholics. By means of it, minds previously impervious to truth have had their eyes opened to the light. They have seen how the man who taunted me with opposition to the circulation of the Bible has himself learned from it that "Christ is a fiction" and the Bible "a crutch;" that he stalks, every Sunday, with bald impiety, into Hopkins' Hall, to teach *these truths* to a Cincinnati audience; and that all the Catholics and Protestants of this city who search the Scriptures, and trust to Christ for salvation, indulge illusory expectations of happiness, follow false lights, and lean but on broken reeds. Now I have placed, disregarding personal insult, his startling impieties, in their native deformity, before the public, so that none may be deceived by him but those that choose to be deceived. And having thus marked him with the "*fœnum in Cornu,*" I say, not only to Catholic, Protestant, and Christian, but also to Israelite, "*Hunc tu caveto.*"

16th. Calvin not only burned Servetus, but wrote a book to justify the act and to prove that it was lawful so to punish heretics. Aretius, in his book *De Supplicio*, contends that Gentilis was justly put to death by the Calvinistic magistrates of Berne. And Beza undertakes to prove the same thesis, more at length, in his book *De Hereticis a Magistratu Puniendis.* These reformers thought, with Bellarmin and others, that if men were freethinkers, they had to keep their freethinking to themselves, and not disturb the peace of society by broaching new doctrines or false religions.

17th. The word "persequar," in what used to be the bishop's oath, meant only to *pursue with argument,* in which sense the word is frequently used. But it is now twenty years since the Fathers of the Sixth Provincial Council of Baltimore objected to the use of the old formula, which admits of an odious sense, and the new formula is this:

"Ego, N. electus Ecclesiæ N. ab hac hora in antea obediens ero beato Petro Apostolo, sanctæque Romanæ Ecclesiæ, et Beatissimo Patri N. Papæ N. suisque successoribus canonice intrantibus. Papatum Romanum adjutor eis ero ad retinendum et defendendum, salvo meo ordine. Jura, honores, privilegia et auctoritatem sanctæ Romanæ Ecclesiæ, Papæ, et successorum prædictorum, conservare, defendere, promovere curabo."

J. B. PURCELL,
Archbishop of Cincinnati.

FINAL REJOINDER OF REV. THOMAS VICKERS.

(Published in the Cincinnati *Gazette*, December 31, 1867.)

To the Editor of the Cincinnati Gazette:

IF there were any need of excuse for the postponement of my reply to the last archiepiscopal eruption, which appeared in your columns on December 5th, it would, doubtless, be sufficient to say, that all my spare time has been consumed in preparing the whole controversy for publication in a more permanent form. I trust that, by this act, I shall make some slight atonement to the Archbishop for all the mental perturbation of which he has been the victim and I the unhappy cause. Now that he has, "on his side, and *in his own better right* (!), shown what this controversy has settled;" now that he has publicly, solemnly, and with marked emphasis, declared that he is "perfectly satisfied with the result;" now that he boasts of having received "oral and written felicitations from both Protestants and Catholics," in view of this result; now that he is happy in the conviction that, by means of this controversy, "minds previously impervious to truth have had their eyes opened to the light;" now that he triumphs in the proud consciousness of having placed my "startling impieties (!) in their native deformity before the public," it will certainly be a source of peculiar satisfaction and delight to him to learn that I have taken such pains to carry the controversy beyond the limits of mere ephemeral and local interest, to spread abroad the fame of his splendid moral and intellectual heroism, and thus, so far as in me lies, to erect to him *monumentum œre perennius*—a monument more enduring than even *his* brass! At any rate, whatever else may be his feeling, he will certainly perceive that I honor and apply the rule, "*audiatur et altera pars.*"

THE ARCHBISHOP FOLLOWS AN EXAMPLE.

With these preliminary remarks, we will now proceed to notice the salient points of the above-named production. The equanimity of the Archbishop evidently received a somewhat severe shock when he read my opinion as to what the controversy had settled, for he immediately begins to rave about "Punchinello" (I suppose he means *Pulcinella*), "self-glorification," etc., and says that I "forgot all the ignorance, inconsistency, and false statements I had made in my encounter with him," and says, also, in the same breath, "*I shall follow his example!!*" Probably all who read this controversy will agree that, whatever example the Archbishop may have followed in these several directions, he has shown himself an apt scholar. I shall not, however, bandy words with him on these points. Those who are qualified to judge will soon be able to form a well-considered judgment for themselves, without his or my further assistance. In glancing over this whole controversy, which I have before me as I write, I find that I have but one statement to retract. One formal misstatement I did make, and I here formally retract it, viz.: that the *Catholic Telegraph* bore the name of Archbishop Purcell as its principal editor. I say *formal* misstatement, because the Archbishop has not only never denied that he controls its columns, but he has shown very conclusively that he does. With this single exception, I have made no statements but such as I have abundantly substantiated.

AN ARCHIEPISCOPAL MARE'S NEST.

At the laying of the corner-stone of St. John's, I said I had been "chosen to express the sympathy of the American population of our city with the occasion." A little more attention to the ordinary rules of grammar, which I have already several times recommended, would have taught the Archbishop the propriety of reserving such *expectorations* as are contained in the first and second paragraphs of his last reply for a more private occasion. Did I say that I had been chosen *by* the American population of our city, either in convention or out of it? Did I not say expressly in my sermon of October 13th, that I had been chosen by the St. John's Society? What a prodigious waste of rhetoric about Episcopalians, Presbyterians, Baptists, Methodists, and Catholics, whose "credentials" I neither asked nor needed!

"ENDLESS REPETITIONS."

In the Archbishop's eleventh paragraph, where it is exceedingly inconvenient for him to follow me, he says "there is no necessity of following the gentleman in his endless repetitions;" but he is never weary of repeating such puerilities as are contained in the third and fourth paragraphs, concerning the Immaculate Conception and the "freemen of Ohio." Of course, every one knows that his last article was written mainly for home consumption; that is, for the special benefit of his "beloved Catholic flock;" but one would think that even they would, by this time, see through the hollowness of such petty artifices. I neither misrepresented the new dogma, nor was I ignorant of its proper content and import. How could I be, with the Papal bull—"*Ineffabilis*"—before me? Nor did I "dictate" to any man how he should vote at the last election, for I said nothing about it until it was all over.

FREE THINKING AND EVIL THINKING.

I have no heart to discuss at length the utterly dishonest and mendacious character of the sixth and seventh paragraphs; it will be apparent to every one who has read the discussion with attention. I will simply call attention to one or two points, concerning which the Archbishop has made some really startling announcements. In the first place, we are indebted to him for a definition of "free thought." He says, with unwearying (although somewhat wearisome) repetition, that "thought is essentially free;" "God made it free, and no power can chain it;" "neither God nor the Church can enslave it;" "man, if he think not, is man no more," etc. I suppose all this ecclesiastical rhetoric, translated into plain, historical, matter-of-fact language, means simply that Huss and Bruno enjoyed, while the flames were crackling around them, the inestimable and inalienable privilege of unlimited freedom of thought! Certainly, this astounding discovery of the Archbishop's must have cost him many sleepless nights and great expenditure of "midnight oil!"

But, on the other hand, although "men could think and speak as they pleased," "when they thought and spoke what was wrong, the Church had a right *to tell them so*"—"God and the Church forbid man to think evil." To "think evil" means here, in plain and unequivocal language, to think contrary to the will of the Catholic Church, which claims to be the infallible exponent of the will of God. How variable the will of this "immutable" church is may be seen from an admission made by the *Dublin Review*, a magazine so ultramontane in its Catholicism that it openly proclaims the infallibility of the Pope. In an article on the Encyclical and Syllabus, in the April number, 1865, may be found the following words: "How was the doctrine of Our Lady's Immaculate Conception circumstanced during that eventful December of 1854? On the 7th of that month, no Catholic was *permitted* to stigmatize its denial as *unsound;* on the 8th, all Catholics were *required* to regard such denial as *heretical*." Therefore we see that the standard of *right thinking* is liable to constant change; that, in fact, what is right thinking and what wrong thinking, what is good thinking and what evil thinking, depends wholly upon the *whim* of this mutable "immutable" Church. On the 7th of December, 1854, one could declare the Virgin Mary not to have been immaculately conceived without even incurring reproof; on the day following, whoever made such a declaration was "in danger of hell fire"—a heretic and reprobate. The right "to tell men so," when they "think evil," is a euphemism which the Archbishop himself has explained to mean *the right to burn men alive*—a right which, as he expressly says, was not only properly exercised against Bruno by Pope Clement VIII, in the year 1600, but might also be properly exercised against Garibaldi by Pius IX, in the year 1867; and yet the Archbishop has the effrontery to say, again and again, that he is "no advocate of coercion."

Archbishop Purcell's theory of free thought may be summed up in these words: No one—not God and not the Church—could prevent a man from thinking and asserting the dogma of the Immaculate Conception to be, like a good many other dogmas of the Romish Church, an absurdity, or, in the classic language of Gregory XVI, "*insane nonsense;*" but, if he did think and say so, the "holy" Church might burn him for it without any detriment to his freedom of thought! Of course, the Archbishop would be very careful not to undertake the burning process in Cincinnati (even in Garibaldi's case). The punishment here, *and at present*, would be an impotent anathema, hurled from the Cathedral, on the corner of Plum and Eighth, coupled, perhaps, with a foaming denunciation in the *Catholic Telegraph*.

CATHOLIC ANCESTORS.

Another remarkable point which the Archbishop repeatedly makes is the following: "Mr. Vickers, and all who think with him, having had, like us, Catholic ancestors, are bound as much as we are to apologize for their conduct, if apology it needs." I most respectfully decline the honor. Dirty Peter Reverendus ac Eruditissimus Dens, and the still dirtier Holy Father, Alexander VI, were no ancestors of mine, and I by no means feel called upon to apologize for them. On the contrary, I hate and detest all such, ancestors or no ancestors.

And, furthermore, when, in the sixteenth paragraph of his reply, Archbishop Purcell attempts to nullify the effect of my quotations from Bellarmin, Dens, Gregory XVI, and Cardinal Pacca, by showing that Calvin, Aretius, and Beza also asserted that it was lawful to punish heretics, I wish to remind him of two things: first, I have never undertaken to defend the Protestant Church against the charge of persecution for opinion's sake, as he has done in the case of the Catholic Church; secondly, Calvin, Aretius, and Beza did not, like Gregory XVI and Cardinal Pacca, live in the nineteenth century, nor were their treatises on the punishment of heresy adopted, within the present century, by any body of Protestant ministers as "the best works and the safest guides in theology," as was the "*Theologia*" of Dens by the Catholic clergy of Dublin, in the year 1808. In general, I may remark, concerning all the Archbishop's tirades against the persecuting spirit of Protestantism, that they would sound better and have more weight if they came from another source.

Loripedem rectus derideat, Æthiopem albus.
Quis tulerit Gracchos de seditione quaerentes?
Quis coelum terris non misceat, et mare coelo,
Si fur displiceat Verri, homicida Miloni?
Clodius accuset moechos, Catilina Cethegum?

THE TRUE RELIGION.

In the sixth paragraph there is a somewhat remarkable instance of that "reticence," which the Archbishop says is so foreign to him. He says: "I maintain, with the Pope, it is a damnable error to teach that Paganism or idolatry is true, that Mormonism or Mohammedanism is true," etc. Is it not also a *damnable error* to teach that Episcopalianism, Presbyterianism, Methodism—in fact, any other *ism* but Catholicism is true? Was the Archbishop thinking of the "oral and written felicitations" when he omitted these from his list?

CHURCH AND STATE.

The readers of this controversy have already had so many brilliant archiepiscopal combinations of grammar, logic, and morals, that they will hardly be surprised at any thing new in this direction, however startling. Perhaps, however, they will be interested to see, in syllogistic form, the substance of what the Archbishop has said on the union of Church and State. Here it is:

1. "It is an error to maintain that the Church *ought* to be separated from the State, and the State from the Church."

Archbishop Purcell says: "I do not want a union of Church and State—I deprecate such a union."

Therefore, Archbishop Purcell, according to his own showing, maintains an error.

2. "It is an error to maintain that the Church *ought* to be separated from the State, and the State from the Church;" that is, Church and State *ought* to be united.

Archbishop Purcell says: "I do not want a union of Church and State—I deprecate such a union."

Therefore, *Archbishop Purcell, according to his own showing, does not want, deprecates, what ought to be.*

Now, either the Archbishop is satisfied with these conclusions, or the bald declaration (published in the *Telegraph*, of October 16), that he did not want a union of Church and State, but deprecated such a union, was a subterfuge, intended to convey a wrong impression, and thus to deceive his readers.

THE BIBLE.

The ravings of Archbishop Purcell, in his last and previous replies, concerning my views of the Bible, are utterly unworthy of notice; either from intentional wickedness or from utter incapacity to understand them, he so distorts and disfigures them, that no sane man would recognize them again. I will, however, here say, for his special information, that should he desire to preach from my pulpit some Sunday, he will find on the desk "the whole Bible," and not the "emasculated (!), mutilated" Scriptures, about which he makes such a pother, and he will be at liberty to interpret or misinterpret it as he chooses, provided that he does not compel those who listen to him to accept his exegesis. Furthermore, when the Archbishop *proceeds to place, and really places*, "a copy of the whole Bible in every Catholic home," and does not merely boast of what he *"proposed"* or *"proposes"* to do, there will be no more occasion for complaints, such as I have personally heard, during the progress of this discussion, from members of *his* "beloved Catholic flock"—that they are not allowed to read the Bible. Let the Archbishop look to it—he is abundantly able—and not wait for some Protestant Bible Society to do it for him.

THE JESUITS ONCE MORE.

I have already had such frequent occasion to point out the equivocations and subterfuges of the Archbishop, that the work has become disgusting to me. Still, there are a few more cases to be noticed, and one of these concerns the Jesuits. At one time he asserts that the Jesuits "take no unconditional vows;" that "the doors and windows are open, and they may leave" whenever they please; now he finds it convenient to let us infer (what we already knew) that it is only the "postulants," or novices and scholastics, who are allowed to leave; but when, after studying the constitutions, where they learn that they are to have no will of their own, but to become as a stick (*baculus*), a corpse (*cadaver*), in the hands of the Superior; when, after this, they take the solemn vow of obedience, there is no escape, except as the criminal escapes from the penitentiary. And what does the Archbishop say when I ask him, before praising too highly the morality of the Jesuits, to look into three Jesuit manuals of morals which I name to him? He says he will not follow me, where I seem so anxious to lead, "into the discussion of immoralities so falsely attributed to the writings of Catholic societies or theologians!" Now the three works I named, and from which I quoted the beginnings of three sentences in the original Latin, not daring to translate their disgusting obscenity, were not only *all written by men eminent in the Society of Jesus,* but were *all issued with the express approbation of the "holy" Church,* and were *all intended for the use of young students as guides to the duties of the future pastoral office, and particularly to the duties of the confessional!*

THE ARCHBISHOP AND THE ENCYCLICAL.

It is very evident that the Archbishop is in some trepidation as to his position toward the Encyclical and Syllabus. The contradiction is so glaring that all his attempts to gloss it over only make the matter worse, as I have shown in regard to the union of Church and State. He took very good care to make no reply to the letter of Mr. Paul Mohr, in which his relation to the "Apostolic See" was discussed with such merciless perspicuity. Of course, as I have already said, I can only congratulate Archbishop Purcell if he honestly differs from documents so utterly subversive of the welfare of the individual and of society, as I take the Encyclical and Syllabus to be, but I abhor and detest the foul hypocrisy which, bitterly hating the whole foundation on which modern society and modern science rest, seeks, by cunning temporization, and artful tergiversation, to gain a firm foothold there where an open and straightforward course would subject it to universal scorn and contempt.

"THE HIATUS."

When Archbishop Purcell said that "the *hiatus*," in my letter of November 22, could be filled "satisfactorily to every candid mind," with answers contained in his letter of November 13, he probably did it in the hope that the public had already forgotten what he did say; at any rate, he himself either no longer had any distinct remembrance of the contents of said letter, or he uttered a deliberate falsehood. I refer "candid minds" to the letters in question. And even now, when the

Archbishop pretends to answer "as categorically, as pertinently, as closely to the question as human language can answer," in order "that I may understand how far he is from reticence or concealment," does he answer the questions I asked him? *Not one of them!* But he *forges* a question I never did ask him; gives an answer to the same which is full of historical perversion, and thus his readers are led astray again.

"SAINT" PETER DE ARBUES.

Although I asked an entirely different question, which the Archbishop did not see fit to answer—namely, whether he *personally* had any thing to do with the canonization of a certain bloody inquisitor—he now volunteers the information that he " believes the saints canonized by the immortal and saintly Pio Nono, in 1867, *deserve the honor!*" Now, I have the decree of canonization before me, and the name of Don Pedro Arbues de Epila is the second on the list of new saints. Perhaps the character of this very man, coupled with the indorsement which he receives at the hands of Archbishop Purcell, will give us some clue to the quality of the Archbishop's own moral judgment.

It is well known that the pretext on which the Inquisition in Spain began its diabolical work was, that among many of the Spanish Jews who, in the year 1391, had been *compelled* by the Church to abandon their ancestral faith, there was still a secret attachment to the religion of their fathers. This was, of course, horrible and not to be endured. After having been introduced into the other Spanish provinces, the Inquisition was, finally, in the year 1480, introduced into the province of Arragon, and here it was that Arbues distinguished himself as one of the most pitiless of the inquisitors. Moreover, the Inquisition appeared at that time in its most hateful and immoral form, namely, as a financial resource, for the royal exchequer was to be enriched by the fortunes of all who were declared guilty. Neither the names of the accusers, nor the accusations themselves, were communicated to the accused; confessions were pressed out of them by the most excruciating tortures, and thousands were burned alive. The persecution extended even to the posterity of the condemned; that is to say, persons who had long been dead were condemned for heresy, and their children were, in consequence, deprived of their property and declared infamous. The people were driven to desperation; an attack was made on Arbues, the chief sinner, who received a deadly wound and died shortly afterward. The authority for these facts is not an enemy of the Church, but the Grand Inquisitor Paramo, whose work: *De origine et progressu officii sanctae inquisitionis* (Madrid, 1598), was the first history of the Inquisition based upon the archives.

Now, Archbishop Purcell is continually declaiming against me because I rake the "kennels of history," as he calls it, to prove that the Catholic Church not only does not tolerate freedom of thought, but persecutes it wherever she finds it, according to the nature and extent of her control over the secular power. He first gives us to understand that persecution is wholly foreign to the Church, and then says that, even if she ever did persecute, Protestants are just as much bound to apologize for it as he; that, in other words, we are equally answerable for the crimes of a common ancestry. Does Archbishop Purcell, in this individual instance, mean to say that Protestants (and perhaps Jews, also) ought to rejoice in the canonization of Don Pedro Arbues, and say that he "deserves the honor?" Is this the archiepiscopal form of "apology" for the want of enlightenment in former ages?

I am afraid simple-minded people will be inclined to lay aside all euphemisms, and say that when, "after mature deliberation" (*matura deliberatione praehabita*), after having "often implored the divine assistance" (*Divina ope saepius implorata*), and "with the advice of the Venerable Brethren of the Holy Roman Church, Cardinals, Patriarchs, Archbishops, and Bishops assembled in Rome" (*de Venerabilium Fratrum Nostrum Sanctae Romanae Ecclesiae Cardinalium, Patriarchorum, Archiepiscoporum et Episcoporum in Urbe existentium consilio*), Pius IX, who claims to represent the Universal Catholic Church, proclaims the bloody villain Arbues to be a saint, this is a more authoritative and more significant manifestation of the real animus of that Church than any utterance in favor of the liberty of conscience made by a mere subordinate prelate, even if such utterance were meant in good faith; but when Archbishop Purcell, after all his vaunting declamation, comes forward and boldly asserts that Arbues is worthy of saintship, they will say he simply eats his own words, and again admits (as already in the case of Bruno and Garibaldi) that every thing he has said in opposition to my original thesis is false.

BRUNO *alias* BRUNI.

The last word of the Archbishop concerning Bruno

confirms a suspicion which his first utterance in regard to him awakened in my mind. It is now perfectly evident that, when Bruno's name was first introduced into the controversy, the Archbishop rushed to the first best encyclopædia for information. This is the explanation of the childish and ridiculous stories about Bruno's quarreling with Calvin and Beza, and being obliged to fly from Geneva, his turning Lutheran, and his banishment from Wittenburg, etc. This is also the reason why De Feller must be elevated, by archiepiscopal authority, to the rank of an historian, and, indeed, of a "most reliable" one; doubtless the *Biographie Universelle* will henceforth be regarded in the "archdiocese" of Cincinnati, if nowhere else, as final authority in matters of history. This is also the explanation of that new specimen of the Archbishop's erudition, that Bruno's "Italian name" was Bruni. Concerning this latter point, I would simply say in passing, that if the Archbishop is desirous of consulting the *only* existing Italian edition of Bruno's works, he will find the same in my library, and the title is as follows: "*Opere Giordano Bruno.*"

AN ARCHIEPISCOPAL ANTI-CLIMAX.

In the fourteenth paragraph the Archbishop is again jubilant over something which he considers "caps the climax of Mr. Vickers' ignorance, inconsistency, and lack of logic," and is so blind as not to see that the passage he cites from my reply of November 22 was intended as a *persiflage* of *his* ratiocination. I trust the Archbishop, who took the liberty of playing upon my name, will not take it amiss if I designate the same as the *argumentum ad porcellum*, and ask him to make a note of it for future use. The plain grammatical and logical import of what I said was this: that it would be, historically and psychologically, just as allowable to vindicate to the Catholic Church all the credit for Leahy's murder as to vindicate to her all the credit for Bacon's science and Luther's learning. To mention but a single fact: Who made it possible for Luther to translate the books of the Old Testament into his mother tongue? Did the Catholic Church? History tells us that the "holy" Church, instead of teaching her monks Hebrew, was, at that very time, inveighing against Reuchlin, as in league with the devil, because he sought to revive the study of the Hebrew language and literature. Luther learnt his Hebrew mainly from a Jew! Does the Archbishop now comprehend the import of what I said? If he does not, I will give him the benefit of a still further example, and tell him that any reasoning which, in accordance with the laws of history and psychology, would make "Christ" "deserving of homage of men and angels for the teachings of the inspired Evangelists and Apostles," would also "make him responsible for the treason and suicide of Judas," providing the terms "deserving of homage" and "responsible" are taken to be equivalents. While again recommending to him the study of some elementary treatise on grammar and logic, let me also suggest the propriety of his taking some lessons in style from Horace or somebody else, before he again speaks of "marking" a person "with the *fœnum in cornu*." However, I can not but thank him for the compliment he pays me in the quotation of these words, blundering and unintentional though it is, and meant to be exactly the reverse: "*Fœ-*

num habet in cornu; longe fuge"—that is to say, "I have found him to be a dangerous opponent; *it is better to keep a long way out of his reach.*" "*Hunc tu*, ROMANE, *caveto!*" is the genuine text of Horace, which the Archbishop took care to "emasculate."

THE BISHOP'S OATH.

The concluding paragraph of the Archbishop's reply contains two specimens of polemical unfairness (to use an expression altogether too mild to suit the case) which completely eclipse all his previous prevarications. In the first place, he asserts, with startling audacity, that the verb *persequi*, "in what used to be the Bishop's oath, meant only to *pursue with argument*, in which sense the word is frequently used." I am sorry to be obliged again to propose an unpleasant alternative to the Archbishop: either he uttered an unconscious untruth, or he did not know what he was talking about. Every man, who knows any thing at all about the Latin language, knows that the verb *persequi, unmodified*, as it occurs in the formula which I cited, *never means, and never can mean*, to "*pursue with argument*," and I defy the Archbishop to produce any Latin author by whom it is so used.

"But," secondly, the Archbishop says, "it is now twenty years since the Fathers of the Sixth Provincial Council of Baltimore objected to the use of the old formula, *which admits of an odious sense.*" So, it does really "admit of" an odious sense? And the "Fathers of the Sixth Provincial Council" *objected* to it? And so it seems, after all, according to the Archbishop's own showing, that down to the year 1846, every bishop (even in this country) swore on his bended knees, and with his hands resting on the Gospel (which teaches us to love our enemies, and to do good to them that hate us), *swore a solemn oath to persecute and assail all heretics to the extent of his power!* In the first place, *the word has no such odious meaning;* and, in the second place, *we objected to it because it has!* O, immaculate logician!

But, still further, what did the Archbishop mean by the phrases, "What used to be the Bishop's oath," and "new formula"? There must be something wrong in his chronology, as well as in the various other departments I have mentioned. His so-called "*new* formula" appears in the proceedings of the Sixth Provincial Council of Baltimore, held in 1846, and my *old* formula, "what *used to be* the Bishop's oath," appears in the *Pontificalia Romana, issued by the Church itself,* and printed in Mechlin in 1855! So the *old* formula is actually *newer, by nine years,* than the "*new*" one! Or, does the one, holy, *immutable* Catholic Church require one thing on the continent of Europe, and another and different thing in the United States?

We are not left without explanation. And this time I have no alternative to offer. This time the Archbishop is manifestly and palpably dishonest. He says the Sixth Baltimore Council objected to the "old formula," and then pretends to give the oath now required, introducing it with the words, *"And the new formula is this."* Now, inasmuch as I find the name of "JOANNES BAPTISTA, *Episcopus Cincinnatensis,*" among those who subscribed to the decrees of the Council in question, and as the so-called "new" formula is the one now used in this country in the consecration of bishops, he must know precisely what that formula is; and yet what does he do? He says, "Here is the new formula," and *intentionally conceals more than three-fourths of it!* He conceals, especially, the passage which proves conclusively that there is no essential difference between the "new" and the "old." I shall take the liberty of communicating the whole, with a translation. What is omitted by the Archbishop is included in brackets, and the passage in small capitals is the one just alluded to. It is found in the reports of the Baltimore Councils, entitled, *Concilia Provincialia, Baltimori habita ab anno* 1829 *usque ad annum* 1849 (2d. ed., Balt., 1851, pp. 258, 259), and is as follows:

Ego, N., electus Ecclesiæ N., ab hac hora in antea obediens ero beato Petro Apostolo, sanctæque Romanæ Ecclesiæ, et Beatissimo Patri N., Papæ N., suisque successoribus canonice intrantibus. Papatum Romanum adjutor eis ero ad retinendum et defendensum, salvo meo ordine. Jura, honores, privilegia et auctoritatem sanctæ Romanæ Ecclesiæ, Papæ, et successorum prædictorum, conservare, defendere, promovere curabo. [REGULAS SANCTORUM PATRUM, DECRETA, ORDINATIONES, SEU DISPOSITIONES ET MANDATA APOSTOLICA, TOTIS VIRIBUS OBSERVABO, ET FACIAM AB ALIIS OBSERVARI. *Vocatus ad synodum, veniam, nisi præpeditus fuero canonica præpeditione. Apostolorum limina singulis decenniis personaliter per me ipsum visitabo; et Beatissimo Patri Nostro, N., ac successoribus præfatis rationem de toto meo pastorali officio, ac de rebus omnibus ad meæ Ecclesiæ statum, ad cleri et populi disciplinam, animarum*

I, N., bishop-elect of the Church of N., will, from this time forward, be obedient to the blessed Apostle Peter, and to the Holy Roman Church, and to the Most Holy Father N., Pope N., and to his successors, canonically instituted. I will assist them in upholding and defending the Roman Papacy, saving my own order. I will take care to preserve, defend, and promote the rights, honors, privileges, and authority of the Holy Roman Church, of the Pope, and his aforesaid successors. [THE RULES OF THE HOLY FATHERS, THE DECREES, ORDINANCES OR DISPOSALS, AND APOSTOLIC MANDATES, I WILL OBSERVE WITH MY WHOLE STRENGTH, AND CAUSE THEM TO BE OBSERVED BY OTHERS. Called to the synod, I will come, unless prevented by a canonical hinderance. The threshold of the apostles I will visit, in my own person, every ten years,

ARCHISBHOP PURCELL TO REV. THOMAS VICKERS.

(Published in the *Catholic Telegraph*, January 15, 1868.)

Rev. Mr. Vickers occupied two columns and a quarter of the Cincinnati *Gazette*, December 31st, with a final rejoinder to the undersigned. It will take many a final rejoinder before the gentleman can convince any man of sense that he has answered the Archbishop. To use one of his favorite vulgarisms, his last "eruption" or "expectoration," however foul the stomach, or deep the cesspool from which it rises, may be characteristic of the man, or savory to his sympathizers, but it is mere verbiage, without reason, truth, or argument. His tiresome repetitions must be an apology for mine, which I hope will not be found tiresome. His first expectoration is that our Lord and only Savior, Jesus Christ, was no more than a "theological fiction"—a myth, or mere creature at best, and not God—and that, consequently, the Jews who crucified him for calling himself God were not guilty of deicide. They only illustrated *free thought* when they concluded in their own minds he was a blasphemer; *free speech*, when they cried out "Away with him!" and *free action*, when they put him to an ignominious and a cruel death.

Second expectoration. "The Bible is but a crutch." This sacred oracle of heaven, this authentic revelation of the Divine will, this dearest charter of human rights and aspirations, but a crutch, to be cast away in the name of that reason which, while it was man's only guide, filled the earth with idolatry, ignorance, and crime!

Third expectoration. "Jesus made his grandmother bring his own mother into the world without due process of nature." The squirming, the wriggling, the twisting and turning, with which he vainly essays to turn attention from the ignorance betrayed by this "eruption" is truly comical.

Fourth expectoration. The anathema of despotism hurled at the heads of all who dared think for themselves in the choice of candidates at the late election.

Fifth expectoration. "That the Catholic Church forbids the people to read the Bible." For this false and injurious statement he has never had the honesty to say *peccavi*, our proof to the contrary notwithstanding.

Sixth expectoration. The Catholic Church forbids "free thought." To this we replied that neither God, who made thinking essential to mind, so that it is impossible to conceive otherwise of the mind than as a thinking principle; nor the Church, which neither could nor would change the essence of mind, forbids free thought. But *free* thought and voluntary *bad* thought, *free* speech and *bad* speech, *free* actions and bad ones, are different things; and that the Church can not, any more than God, allow men to think, to say, or to do evil, is clear from the 9th, 10th, 11th, and 12th verses of the seventeenth chapter of Deuteronomy, where God commands all, under penalty of death, to give up their own, until then, free thought and judgment, and abide by the sentence of the priest and judge. Mr. Vickers has not seen fit to tell us what he thinks of God Almighty for this. It is evidently an interdicting of *bad* thought by him who endowed man with *free* thought. And if God, without ceasing to be immutable and just, could so restrict his own gift as to render it not hurtful, but salutary, to man, I ask if the Church, which holds the place of God on earth, does wrong when, leaving man to think freely, she forbids him to think badly? To this reasoning Mr. Vickers made no answer. Now, there are only two answers which he could have made:

1st. That this was under the old dispensation—no longer binding on Christians. This we may peremptorily deny. It was only the ritual portion of the Old Testament that was abrogated by the New, the Decalogue and moral law remaining the same. 2d. He may answer that the Church does not hold the place of God on earth. This, also, we deny. The gentleman says he has the Bible—the complete, unmutilated, unemasculated Bible—on the desk, if there be one, in Hopkins' Hall. Has he, then, never read in it the ordinance of Christ, That he who will not hear the Church (but prefer to her thoughts his own) is to be reputed as "the heathen and the publican" (Matt. xviii: 27); that it is not against the individual, but against the Church, he promised the gates of hell would never prevail" (Matt. xvi: 18); that to the Church his own and his Holy Spirit's perpetual assistance was promised: "They who hear her, hear himself; they who despise her, despise him and the Father who sent him" (Luke x: 16); that he made her the "pillar and ground of the truth" (1 Tim. iii: 15); that, when ascending into heaven, "he left to her the ministry of reconciliation" (2 Cor. v: 18); that to the Church he gave authority and commandment "to teach all nations until the consummation of ages," imposing on them the obligation to believe her? And what is all this but proof from the New Testament that the Church does hold the place of God on earth—that she is the "one fold of the one Shepherd" (John x: 16); and that, as in the first days of Christianity, so now and forever he daily "adds to her such as shall be saved" (Acts ii: 47)? Far from disparaging reason, the Church teaches that, though free as the ocean in her domain, she is not, any more than the ocean, illimitable. There is a barrier which, in her wildest excesses, she must respect, breaking her proud swelling waves on the shore where God has written the irrevocable words, "No farther" (Job xxxviii: 11).

Seventh expectoration. The Archbishop's Pastoral on the Encyclical and the Syllabus is in contradiction with the teachings of the Church; he will surely incur the displeasure of the Pope; he is threatened with the "Inquisition." It is passing strange that this "mare's nest" should have been discovered only by Mr. Vickers. The Archbishop knows grammar, logic, ethics, theology a little too well to heed the warnings or to share the fears of the pope of Hopkins' Hall.

Eighth expectoration. St. Cyprian denied the Pope's supremacy. I have quoted irrefragable proof to the contrary.

Ninth expectoration: St. Augustine and Aquinas counselled the burning of heretics. I have quoted their own words to show, that while they agreed with God and the sacred writers of the Old and New Testament, that heresy was one of the deadly sins, they advocated lenity to the convicted. Nothing can be plainer or stronger than their language to this effect, but the wilfully blind will not see when the sun shines.

Tenth expectoration. The definition of the Immaculate Conception on the 8th of December, 1854. On this subject the gentleman must allow me to say that he absolutely assumes the infallibility of his logic, and swells like the frog in the fable. "On the 7th of December, 1854," he says, "one could declare the Virgin Mary not to have been immaculately conceived without even incurring reproof; on the day following, whoever made such a declaration was in danger of hell fire—a heretic, a reprobate." Yes, it was even so. The day before the definition of a dogma, it was not *heresy* to deny it; the day after its definition it was heresy. An *opinion* might have been more or less unsound, untenable, unreasonable; but when the supreme court, the infallible tribunal which God had established to decide controversies that would otherwise have been interminable, had once authoritatively spoken, it was no longer an opinion, but a doctrine of faith. It was thus that the precedent and justification of what was done in Rome, on the memorable 8th of December, 1854, were found in the first, the model Council of Jerusalem, when, on occasion of the discussion that agitated the Church at Antioch, "Paul and Barnabas determined, and some others of the other side, to go up to the apostles and ancients at Jerusalem about this question." And when *opinions* and arguments had been heard and considered by the apostles and ancients, and there was much disputing, which ceased when Peter and James had spoken, the decree was issued, commencing with the words: "It hath seemed good to the Holy Spirit and to us." (Acts xv: 28.) Before the rendition of this solemn decision, they who held a free opinion "incurred no reproof;" after its rendition it was no longer a free opinion, and they who obstinately persisted in it, resisted at once the Holy Ghost and the Church. And this decision of the apostles and ancients was no "whim." And the Church that rendered it was not mutable, but steadfast and immutable in her adherence to truths, misunderstood, it might have been by some, but now by divine providence made clear and imperative to all.

Need, then, intelligent Christians be informed that it was in this very manner that the canon of the Bible, the books of Scripture, were determined. It was the Church that decided the controversy, which had lasted *three hundred years*, with regard to the books entitled to be called canonical. She separated the wheat from the chaff, the true from the false, the genuine from the spurious, and when she had done this, she forfeited not her claim to be the immutable Church of an immutable Savior-God. Was it a "whim" on the part of Jehovah when, from non-creating, He became creating? when he revealed doctrines never revealed before, and proclaimed laws which then, for the first time, became obligatory?

Eleventh expectoration. Bruno and Garibaldi once more. Yet they both, in their way and to the utmost, made war, not on the religion alone, but on the lawful possessions, the peaceful subjects, and the life of the

Pope, and by those acts forfeited their lives to the laws.

Twelfth expectoration. He says—and I quote his words, that all who read this controversy may know from his own foul pen who and what he is—"The ravings of Archbishop Purcell are utterly unworthy of notice, either from intentional wickedness, or from utter incapacity to understand them;" *his* views of the Bible—and he proceeds to aver that he has *"personally heard, during the progress of this discussion, from members of 'his beloved Catholic flock,' that they are not allowed to read the Bible."* This I here pronounce a barefaced falsehood. And if Mr. Vickers does not give the names of the members of my "beloved flock" who have made this false statement, I now pronounce him the author of it. He says "It has become disgusting to me to point out the equivocations and subterfuges of the Archbishop." Let us see what equivocations and subterfuges will extricate him from the foregoing.

Thirteenth expectoration. He would rather have no ancestry than such as I have named—he acknowledges none like Peter Dens and others who advocate persecution for opinions. Well he may repudiate all past ages except the nineteenth if he please, and claim to have been born without due process of nature. But who have been the persecutors, or the persecuted in the nineteenth century? By whom was civil and religious liberty first proclaimed in the colony of Maryland or the United States of America? By whom in the United States, and in the nineteenth century, have convents, churches, and private dwellings been burned, and galling school-taxes imposed? *Not by Catholics.* It is "disgusting" to me to allude to those persecutions of Catholics, but let the blame fall where it is deserved. I would not willingly rake up those kennels.

Fourteenth expectoration. His spite against the Jesuits. He tires not in his abuse of them, their manual, and their morals. I repeat, postulant, novice, scholastic, or professed, the chain of his own will is the only one that binds him to the society. He is as free to leave it as the members of any firm, corporation, church, or partnership is to leave his previous association; and in this he "escapes not like a criminal from the penitentiary." The thought could hardly have entered into another mind than Rev. Thomas Vickers'. The Jesuit! Why he will expectorate more cacochymy than would fill the great tun of Heidelberg before he will render to astronomy, to the Pagans, the Indians, the negroes, to literature, to patriotism, to morality, the thousandth part of what has been done by De Vico, Secchi, Claver, Francis Xavier, Marquette, Brebeuf, Father De Smet, Bishop Carroll, or the Jesuits of Cincinnati, New York, St. Louis, Georgetown, Spring Hill, or Baltimore.

Fifteenth expectoration. Arbues, who was himself murdered! Why does he not read the History of the Spanish Inquisition, by the Count de Maistre, as we have counseled him to do. He will then see that it had a royal, not an ecclesiastical, origin, and that the very life of the Spanish nation was imperiled by the Moors and Jews. Read Washington Irving and the fall of the Alhambra; read the History of the Knights of Malta, of the Corsairs of Algiers, of the life-long struggle of Christianity with Mohammedanism, and you will see what European nations had to do, to dare, to suffer, in the conflict with Islamism, Judaism, and wild sectaries, and then, perhaps, you will discover, if your mind is not incurably warped by prejudice, that it was the instinct of self-preservation that originated the Inquisition. Of its abuses I am no more an advocate than you profess to be of the persecutions of Catholics by Protestants, of which I could draw a harrowing picture from authentic history.

But as I write to give useful information to those who seek it in sincerity, and not for Mr. Vickers, whom many consider unworthy of notice, I must here take occasion to quote from the latest church history a just and truthful appreciation of the origin, object, spirit, and operation of the tribunal of the Inquisition. Speaking of the decree promulgated by Pope Lucius III, in the Council of Verona, A. D. 1184, against Western Manichæism, at the formal request of the Emperor Frederick, the lords of his court, and Christian rulers, Darras (Ch. Hist., vol. 3, pp. 233 and 234) says: "Both the principle and the action of the Inquisition have been deeply calumniated by writers hostile to the Church. It has been described as, in principle, an encroachment of the spiritual power, upholding by armed force the teachings which concern only the conscience and spiritual rule. Its action has been taxed with a refinement of cruelty truly barbarous, and altogether unheard of in the treatment of other crimes. The hour of justice has at length arrived, and these odious charges have vanished before the deeper and more impartial study of historic facts. The Church, clothed in the middle ages with a protective power, was, in duty, bound to guard public order and the peace of society, equally threatened by the heretics, whose blows were aimed both at civil and religious institutions. A weak indulgence at such a moment would have proved the Church false to its mission and unworthy of the people's confidence. As a spiritual society, using first but spiritual weapons against the enemies of order and religion, when her censures were disregarded, at the formal request of the emperors and princes of Christendom, she gave up to civil justice the rebels she could not subdue. Insurrection, at the present time, falls within the jurisdiction of civil courts alone. In the middle ages the guilty parties enjoyed the guarantee of two jurisdictions; they fell under the hand of civil justice only when they had cast off the merciful intervention of the Church. Time has swept away, in its course, the public law of the middle ages; who shall say that humanity has gained by the change? The sentences decreed by the Inquisition were, indeed, uttered by a civil tribunal. In form, they were such as accorded with the criminal law of the age. Personally we may be moved to pity by the fate of the unfortunate wretches who suffered at a period when civil discord gave birth to scenes of horror unknown even to the ages of barbarism. But inflexible history, the accomplice of no party, rejecting all *a priori* systems, bears unquestionable witness that the punishments of the Inquisition were those inflicted by every tribunal for other crimes. Can we forget that the torture was not abolished in France until the reign of the martyr-king Louis XVI? It might not be too wide of the truth to say that the period which is most ready to weep over the cruel fate of criminals is that in which crime stalks abroad most frequent and most unharmed. Under one name or another, the Inquisition necessarily exists in every community that seeks its own preservation. A community can exist only inasmuch as it watches and punishes all who plot or who attempt its overthrow. But in the middle ages the fundamental law of society was the Catholic faith. This law took precedence of every other. He who was not a Catholic, was not a citizen. The Church, then, by protecting its faith, upheld social order, secured the peace of kingdoms, and defended the supreme law of civilization."

Sixteenth expectoration. De Faller. I know not such an author. This is Mr. Vickers' bad spelling or ignorance. The author of the "Biographie Universelle" is not named De Faller, but De Feller, and he is more reliable in his account of Bruno, or Bruni, than the inventor or inventors of the story about Catholics in Cincinnati being forbidden to read the Bible.

Seventeenth expectoration. Luther and Bacon acquired not—the one his biblical learning, the other his science, in the schools of the Church! Where else did Luther acquire his learning? You answer, he was taught Hebrew by a Jew. But Luther was, a long time, a Catholic, a novice, and for fifteen years an Augustinian monk in his convent before he escaped, if you will, "like a criminal from a penitentiary." He confesses that all that long time he was a good and faithful religious. Then who, in a convent, supplied him with a professor of Hebrew and of other branches of study? The Church, or those whom she had commissioned to teach and to rule the monastery? You falsely assert that Hebrew was a forbidden study. Not in St. Jerome's day, not in Luther's, or in any other's. Reuchlin, nicknamed Smoke, as you have been Fortune-teller or Gypsy, and I Porcellos (and this name was given to one of the ancients for a noble exploit, and not by prophecy to me because I was destined to be Bishop of Porkopolis), studied in the Catholic schools of Germany, France, and Italy, and became an eminently learned man *in one of the Dark Ages*. In Rome he translated a passage of Thucydides for Argyrophilus, pronouncing the Greek with an accent so pure, that his teacher, with a sigh, exclaimed, "*Græcia nostra in exilio transvolavit Alpes.*" Notwithstanding the advantage taken of his disputes with some of the school-men to make him embrace the errors of Luther, he rejected those advances, and died happily in the communion of the Catholic Church, at Hutgart, in 1522, aged sixty-seven years. Thus he is none of yours, and I see not why, spider-like, you suck poison where others find honey.

Eighteenth expectoration. That oath. You get it from our own standard works, even the Baltimore Councils published in America, where the Pope knows we solemnly and truly swear to support the constitution, which, I say again and again, with no apprehension of consequences such as your morbid or malignant brain conjures up, thank God, allows no persecution for conscience' sake. Do not seek to thrust down our throats a theory or a practice that we abhor. Our life is before the world. You reproach us with calumnies; we answer with facts. You flung a wanton insult into the faces of all orthodox Christians, proving yourself as much of a persecutor as you dared be, in a public address. But for this you would, in all probability, have never heard from me, who, as far as I am aware, have never seen, and who do not know you. I waste no midnight oil in answering you; your gas would afford light enough, if I required it. *Il n' y a* seeks its own preservation. A community can exist only inasmuch as it watches and punishes all who plot or who attempt its overthrow. But in the middle ages the fundamental law of society was the Catholic faith. This law took precedence of every other. He who was not a Catholic, was not a citizen. The Church, then, by protecting its faith, upheld social order, secured the peace of kingdoms, and defended the supreme law of civilization."

Sixteenth expectoration. De Faller. I know not such an author. This is Mr. Vickers' bad spelling or ignorance. The author of the "Biographie Universelle" is not named De Faller, but De Feller, and he is more reliable in his account of Bruno, or Bruni, than the inventor or inventors of the story about Catholics in Cincinnati being forbidden to read the Bible.

Seventeenth expectoration. Luther and Bacon acquired not—the one his biblical learning, the other his science, in the schools of the Church! Where else did Luther acquire his learning? You answer, he was taught Hebrew by a Jew. But Luther was, a long time, a Catholic, a novice, and for fifteen years an Augustinian monk in his convent before he escaped, if you will, "like a criminal from a penitentiary." He confesses that all that long time he was a good and faithful religious. Then who, in a convent, supplied him with a professor of Hebrew and of other branches of study? The Church, or those whom she had commissioned to teach and to rule the monastery? You falsely assert that Hebrew was a forbidden study. Not in St. Jerome's day, not in Luther's, or in any other's. Reuchlin, nicknamed Smoke, as you have been Fortune-teller or Gypsy, and I Porcellus (and this name was given to one of the ancients for a noble exploit, and not by prophecy to me because I was destined to be Bishop of Porkopolis), studied in the Catholic schools of Germany, France, and Italy, and became an eminently learned man *in one of the Dark Ages.* In Rome he translated a passage of Thucydides for Argyrophilus, pronouncing the Greek with an accent so pure, that his teacher, with a sigh, exclaimed, "*Græcia nostra in exilio transvolavit Alpes.*" Notwithstanding the advantage taken of his disputes with some of the school-men to make him embrace the errors of Luther, he rejected those advances, and died happily in the communion of the Catholic Church, at Hutgart, in 1522, aged sixty-seven years. Thus he is none of yours, and I see not why, spider-like, you suck poison where others find honey.

Eighteenth expectoration. That oath. You get it from our own standard works, even the Baltimore Councils published in America, where the Pope knows we solemnly and truly swear to support the constitution, which, I say again and again, with no apprehension of consequences such as your morbid or malignant brain conjures up, thank God, allows no persecution for conscience' sake. Do not seek to thrust down our throats a theory or a practice that we abhor. Our life is before the world. You reproach us with calumnies; we answer with facts. You flung a wanton insult into the faces of all orthodox Christians, proving yourself as much of a persecutor as you dared be, in a public address. But for this you would, in all probability, have never heard from me, who, as far as I am aware, have never seen, and who do not know you. I waste no midnight oil in answering you; your gas would afford light enough, if I required it. *Il n' y a de quoi.* I now close with an advice to you from the Bible (the Vulgate), for I prefer this sacred to profane quotation (Ps. 33, in our version): *"Prohibe linguam tuam a malo: et labia tua ne loquantur dolum. Diverte a malo et fac bonum. Inquire pacem et persequere eam"*—pursue, not persecute it.

J. B. PURCELL,
Archbishop of Cincinnati.

ROGUES' GALLERY.

(From the *Catholic Telegraph*, January 8, 1867.)

WE learn that a Rogues' Gallery of a certain number of the most noted individuals that, from the eleventh to the eighteenth century, advocated the spoliation of Catholic churches, priests, and institutions, will be exhibited by competent showmen, behind and before the scenes, in Hopkins' Hall, for twenty-one successive Sunday evenings. To give the portraits light and shade, the good Catholics, Christopher Columbus, Copernicus, and Galileo, are to be grouped on the same canvas with the malefactors, Arnold of Brescia, John Huss, Wickliffe, Martin Luther, and others *ejusdem farinæ*. Our criticisms on the pictures as they appear will give spiciness to the columns of the *Catholic Telegraph*, which has considerably increased its subscription list by the scoring given in it to Rev. Thomas Vickers. We know the names of the *Apellas* who are helping Thomas.

ARNOLD OF BRESCIA.

SUBJECT OF REV. MR. VICKERS' FIRST LECTURE AT HOPKINS' HALL—REVIEWED BY ARCHBISHOP PURCELL.

[In the *Catholic Telegraph*, of January 15, 1868.]

WE said in the last issue of this paper, that a rogues' gallery was opened in Hopkins' Hall, and that for twenty-one successive Sunday evenings their photographs were to be exhibited by a showman, or showmen. The first of the series was Arnold of Brescia, a disciple of Abelard, immortalized by Pope and Eloise. In the eleventh century, represented with scandalous effrontery by Rev. Thomas Vickers, as an age of utter darkness, in which an extinguisher was placed on the human mind, and free thought was interdicted and unknown, this famous teacher had at his *free* lectures five thousand scholars. While yet a layman, he was the doctor, *a la mode*, in Paris, where his head being turned by his vanity and popularity, his heart became the prey of licentious desires, and he was cruelly deprived of his manhood for a shameful intrigue with Eloise, niece of Fulbert, canon of Paris. Having, like Mr. Vickers, wrong notions on the Trinity, which he defended in a book published for that purpose, the treatise was condemned by the Council of Soissons, at which St. Bernard assisted, in 1121. Abelard appealed to the Pope, and was proceeding to Rome, to prosecute his appeal, when Peter, the venerable abbot of Cluny, induced him to enter the monastery, and successfully labored at the double conversion of his mind and heart. Abelard took the monastic habit, and his subsequent conduct, to his death, and his Letters to Eloise, who was then a penitent at the Paraclete, satisfactorily proved the sincerity of his conversion. Having become infirm he was recommended a change of air, and went to the Monastery of St. Marcellus, at Chalons-sur-Saone, where he died happily, at the age of sixty-three years, in 1142.

From a letter written by the abbot to Eloise we learn the interesting particulars of the penitence and the occupation of Abelard for the two years he passed at Cluny. After highly commending the piety and erudition of the abbess, he says of Abelard: "I do not recollect to have ever seen any one equal to him in humility of dress and manner. I obliged him to take the first place in our monastic community, but he preferred the last. In the processions in which, according to custom, he walked immediately before me, I could not help admiring the voluntary abasement of a man so highly extolled for learning and talents. He was constantly engaged in study and prayer, and observed continual silence, unless when forced to speak in the conferences and sermons which he delivered to the community. He frequently offered the Holy Sacrifice, and even every day after I had obtained his pardon from the Holy See. In fine, his time was employed in meditating and teaching the truths of religion and philosophy.

At St. Marcellus, one of the most healthy and beautiful places in Burgundy, whither I had sent him for change of air, he continued his studies and exercises of piety, until confined to his bed by his last illness. All the religious of that monastery are witnesses to the devotion with which he made first, his confession of faith, and, next, the confession of his sins, and with what avidity he received the Holy Viaticum."

This edifying portion of Abelard's life is passed over by Mr. Vickers with his characteristic reticence, his shameful suppression of whatever might tend to the honor of a Catholic, or the Church. "Abelard," he summarily tells us, "journeyed to Rome, and died on the way."

"Among the thousands," says Mr. Vickers, "who had sat at his (Abelard's) feet, was Arnold." He imitated Abelard in his errors; he did not imitate him in his repentance. St. Anselm, Archbishop of Canterbury, had chosen the words of Isaiah, "If ye believe not, ye shall not be established." Abelard chose the words, "He who believes quickly is of weak understanding." Now, every Catholic is prepared to admit this as an axiom: He who believes quickly, without knowledge, without prayer for heavenly guidance, without sufficient investigation, without knowing his catechism, which is so assiduously taught in Catholic schools and to converts coming to the Church "is of weak understanding." But mark the commentary and the bad faith of Mr. Vickers. "He means by this that a man can believe only what he understands." Ah! Mr. Vickers, your creed is short enough already, but it will be shorter if you believe only what you can understand. Do you understand God? Yet you believe in him. What mysteries in the Divine being, his eternal existence, his immensity and simplicity, his presence in all places and in every place at once, his mercy and his unchangeableness. If you understood all of God you would be God yourself. As well may you pretend to inclose all the air of heaven, the universe, in your hand, as to comprehend in your little mind the nature and attributes of God. Do you understand the phenomena of your own existence, how soul and body were formed, how they came to be united, how they act in wonderful accord? No, sir, affect not to throw dust in the eyes of your hearers. It will not dishonor your intellect or theirs to confess that there are things innumerable, from the star to the hyssop, which man can not understand, but which he believes. So Abelard confessed, and so did even Arnold, for either must have, like you, abjured his reason to disbelieve them.

Arnold was not long content with holding false theories. He reduced them to practice. Condemned in the General Council of Lateran, in 1139, he took up his abode in Zurich, and infected Switzerland with his errors. These consisted in the rejection of the sacrifice of the mass, prayers for the dead, pedobaptism and the veneration of the Cross. He recommended (and for this he is entitled to his place of first in the Rogues' Gallery) the spoliation of all ecclesiastics, popes, cardinals, monasteries, priests of every degree, and of property. With these avowed principles he returned to Rome where he excited a most formidable sedition, caused the pillaging of the palaces of the cardinals, the assault in which Gerard, cardinal priest of the title of Saint Pudentiana, was dangerously wounded as he was proceeding along the Via Sacra to see the Pope, and was probably the cause of the expulsion of the Holy Father himself from Rome. Nicholas Breakspeare, the only English Pope (Adrian IV), was then elevated to this dignity, in virtue of the Catholic principle which throws open the highest office in her gift to merit when discovered in the most humbly born.

"Arnold's doctrines were finally carried to the Eternal City *and at last she sanctioned them.*" So speaks Mr. Vickers. But how did she sanction them? By the expulsion of the Pope; by the burning and plundering of sanctuaries; by bloodshed and sedition, in which she was excited to a momentary phrenzy by the innovator. But at length the senators, unable longer to resist the entreaties of both clergy and people, made their submission to the Sovereign Pontiff, in St. Peter's Church, swearing on the holy Gospels to expel Arnold of Brescia and his adherents from the city and territory of Rome; and they kept their word. Frederick Barbarossa had Arnold arrested and delivered up to the Roman Prefect, whom Arnold had had deposed by the mob, and by him he was condemned to death for his crimes, in 1155.

Writers hostile to the Catholic Church, as Darras well observes, may seek to invest the forerunner of modern revolutionists with the halo of martyrdom in the cause of freedom. He aimed at the overthrow of society and order; he fell in the name and by the sword of order and society. When such a man becomes the patron saint of a lecturer, when a disturber of the public peace, a violent disorganizer, is exhibited as a light to the world, it is the devil that holds the candle.

Mosheim, who, like Mr. Vickers, is always ready to canonize whoever is an enemy to the Catholic faith, says (untruly) that Arnold was a man of immense erudition, but of a turbulent and impetuous character. That his principles were reprehensible only inasmuch as he carried them too far and executed them with a degree of vehemence which was as criminal as it was imprudent; and he falsely adds that he was crucified. This sensational circumstance, Mr. Vickers has the merit of not repeating. His punishment was bad enough, but it was according to the barbarous spirit of the age, such as was elsewhere meted out to the treasonable and the seditious. Mr. Vickers, who, in his lectures and communications shows the fiercest spirit of the tribe of persecutors of former times, pretends that Garibaldi was not, any more than Arnold, deserving of death for his invasion of the States of the Church and the profanation of churches and altars. Does he then consider that Booth, the murderer of President Lincoln, and the assassins of Mr. Seward, unjustly perished?

WICKLIFFE.

SUBJECT OF REV. THOMAS VICKERS' SECOND LECTURE AT HOPKINS' HALL—REVIEWED BY ARCHBISHOP PURCELL.

(In the *Catholic Telegraph*, of January 22, 1868.)

The lecturer, as we find him reported in the *Commercial*, of January 6th, began with devotional exercises. It is evident that during these and after them, he was neither overly devout nor particularly self-possessed, for his opening sentences betray a singular incoherency. Here they are, textually: "About the time of Edward III, John Wickliffe was born. Little is known of John Wickliffe's history till he is found a student of Oxford. It is generally agreed that he was born in 1324." Now, in the name of *lucidus ordo*, why begin by telling us he was born *about the time* of Edward III, and then, after an intercalary sentence, coming back, gravely, if not comically, to state that by general agreement he was born in 1324? But this was only a pardonable confusion of ideas.

When it suits the purpose of the lecturer, he forgets what he had said of the unredeemed darkness of the middle ages, and extols the learning that shone through the fabulous gloom. "He very early," says Mr. Vickers, "made his name famous as one thoroughly versed in all the learning of those times—famous among the distinguished men who were educated in the celebrated (Merton) college."

And he qualifies Wickliffe's reply to the pamphlet of an anonymous monk, on a certain alleged Papal usurpation, as "a powerful production." It strikes us that the lecturer's memory or his consistency is here sadly at fault, and that thoughtful hearers must have marveled how all this learning and that crowd of distinguished men and scholars could have issued from the bosom of such deep Cimmerian darkness.

An irrepressible smile will grace the reader's, or the hearer's, features at the next piece of "interesting and instructive" information vouchsafed by the lecturer, when, coming to the written or oral lectures of Wickliffe, he proclaims that "God himself follows the right because it is right," and that "moral laws are immutable." If this be not *bathos*, we know not where else to seek it. If Oxford men at that day could have taught no better, we should have had reason to exclaim, in the witty sarcasm of Mrs. Siddons, at a late period

"Oxford no more; now Cowford be thy name,
Since thou hast produced such calves—to thy eternal shame."

Without enlightening his audience as to the distinctive errors or theories of Wickliffe, he tells us he was condemned by the University of Oxford, and that the Pope, to whom he had appealed, issued a bull declaring his doctrine heretical, so that he withdrew to his parish at Lutterworth, where he spent his days in retirement and in writing defenses of his doctrines.

Wickliffe opposed the doctrine of Transubstantiation; but, nevertheless, he was struck with apoplexy, during the celebration of Mass, on Innocents' (Holy Innocents') day, 1385, and so finished his career.

The infidel historian Hume seems to have known more than Rev. Mr. Vickers of Wickliffe's errors. "He had the honor," says Mr. Hume, "of being the first to call in question the doctrines which had universally passed as certain and undisputed for so many ages. They were nearly the same with those propagated in the sixteenth century." What better vindication of the truth of the Catholic Church—what better refutation of the falsehoood of the reformed, deformed innovations—could the hand of the infidel have penned?

Truthful and impartial history teaches us that Wickliffe changed his creed because he had been thwarted in his ambitious projects—first, as to the rectorship of Queen's College, Oxford, and, secondly, in his aspirations to an Episcopal mitre. He then began to declaim against the temporal and spiritual power of the Pope, against the benefices of the clergy, without, however, surrendering his own; that auricular confession was superfluous and unnecessary; that it could not be proved from the Gospel that Christ had instituted the Mass; that a bishop or a priest in mortal sin could not validly baptize, ordain, or consecrate; to which he added many other propositions, subversive alike of civil order and ecclesiastical jurisdiction. From the pestilential seed thus sown broadcast by the herald of free thought in the fourteenth century sprang the Lollards, whose paternity is candidly, or compulsorily, assigned by Mr. Vickers to Wickliffe. His patron was the Duke of Lancaster, John of Gaunt. His pupils were the itinerant preachers of sedition, John Ball, Wat Tyler, Jack Straw, Tom Millar, and the *hundred thousand insurgents* collected from the rabble of London and its environs, who, in the name of the primitive equality and natural rights of all men—for

> "When Adam delved and Eve span,
> Who was then a gentleman?"—

plundered the goods and burned the houses of the rich, the sober, the industrious, the thrifty, until the Duke of Lancaster was ashamed of his *protégé*, and the strong arm of the law, hastening to the defense of good government, society, and order, crushed out the insurrection. A seventy-four-gun ship might have floated in the blood shed by the followers of Wickliffe in those fearful upheavings of all the worst elements of misguided and degraded humanity. But this was a thousand times better than to have shut up Wickliffe in a monastery, where he could have done no evil! Perhaps Mr. Dickens, when he visits Cincinnati, may be prevailed upon by a committee to favor us with a reading of his own inimitable description of the Lord John Gordon riots as an illustration of that instigated by Wickliffe.

THIRD PORTRAIT IN THE ROGUES' GALLERY AT HOPKINS' HALL.

REVIEWED BY ARCHBISHOP PURCELL.

(In the *Catholic Telegraph*, of January 29, 1868.)

THE man who would judge correctly of historic scenes and actors in by-gone ages must, if he would not deceive himself and others, and do injustice to the past, thoroughly understand the condition of society, the laws and usages, the principles and habits of thought, that were prevalent in those ages. It is owing to an unpardonable disregard of this rule of equity and common sense that the Church and the legislation of the mediæval age are so often misrepresented.

In the first centuries of the Christian era, paganism was identified with all that was oppressive, unjust, and cruel to the followers of the true religion. And the followers of Christ had scarcely overthrown idolatry, when they had to encounter the hostility of the Arian emperors, the Iconoclasts, the Mohammedans; to these succeeded the various forms of persecution of sound doctrine, excited by the subsequent heresies, the Albigenses, the Cathari, the poor men of Lyons, or Puritans, and all that host of seditious and sanguinary sects, whose name is legion, which taught that churchmen had not the same civil rights as others, and that these, as well as kings, princes, and civil rulers of every degree forfeited their authority when they were falsely, or not, accused of having fallen into mortal sin. These were the teachings of the Wickliffites, the Lollards, the Hussites, by them bequeathed to their successors, the innovators of the sixteenth century, which filled a large portion of Germany with ruins and threatened, if unchecked in their impious career, the very existence of society.

That we do not exaggerate in speaking of the errors of Huss and Jerome of Prague in this connection, we here refer to the four propositions by them advanced before the Council of Constance: "1st. The Church is a mystical body, of which Christ is the head; of this Church the just and predestined are the only members, to the exclusion of sinners and the reprobate. Since no one who has been predestined (no matter what his merits or demerits) can be lost, no member (no matter what his vices or his errors) can be separated from the body of the Church; excommunication, therefore, does not exclude from eternal life. Besides, the Pope and the bishops not being empowered to make the distinction (which these audacious sectarians assumed) between the elect and the reprobate, the Church would not cease to subsist even if there were neither Pope nor bishops. 2d. Every action of a virtuous man is good; every action of a sinner is bad; hence civil and religious officers lose their respective authority by the commission of mortal sin, in which case revolt is a duty and a right. 3d. Jesus Christ alone has the power to bind and to loose; this power he did not delegate to the apostles or their successors. 4th. The Scripture is the only rule of faith and conduct. It is radically contrary to the Scripture to restrict the right to preach the Gospel."

Church history vindicates the Council of Constance from the charge of having violated the safe conduct granted to the Bohemian reformers by the Emperor Sigismund. In granting it he had no intention of exempting them from obedience to the decrees of the Council. It was meant to protect them on their journey, and while they remained, unheard, in Constance; during this period they were perfectly free. But when they had got a hearing at the bar of the Council, and enjoyed full liberty to defend their opinions, and these opinions were refuted and condemned, but unretracted, their obstinacy changed their position, and made them amenable, as the open and avowed enemies of religion and society, to the penal legislation then in force. "The philanthropic wail," says Darras, "raised by Lutheranism, and the Voltairian school, over their deserved fate, had been more fittingly uttered over the wretched victims of Hussite errors and the innocent blood which they so plentifully shed." But while the civil and ecclesiastical legislation of the age was charged to protect an essentially Christian and Catholic society, and to regard whatever tended to weaken the faith, or to undermine its foundation, as a crime of high treason against that society, the Catholic Church, or the ecclesiastical legislation, must not be left alone to answer for what was not looked upon as excessive punishment, or for what was executed only by the civil ruler. As St. Augustine, Aquinas, and all the councils had so often decided, the punishment of public crimes belongs immediately in *spiritual matters* to the ecclesiastical tribunals; in temporal concerns, to the civil magistrates. The one brands erroneous theories with the particular censure they deserve; the other inflicts penalties on crimes against the laws of the land.

Now, when in its fifteenth session the Council had condemned the following proposition as subversive of faith and morals, viz.: "A tyrant can and ought, lawfully and meritoriously, to be killed by any vassal or subject, even by stratagem and deceit, notwithstanding any obligation of an oath or covenant made with said tyrant, and this without waiting for the command or sentence of any judge whatsoever," and Huss refused audaciously, in presence of the Emperor, the King of Hungary and the other princes and prelates, to retract the same, glorying, like Booth in the "*sic semper tyrannis*," and proceeded further to call Wickliffe a saint, and asserted that his followers ought, in imitation of Moses, to resort to the use of arms, against the enemies of the truth, Sigismund declared that Huss had come to Constance with a letter of protection from himself, and that he had promised to procure him a public trial. That the same had now had an impartial hearing, and herewith his own pledged royal word had been redeemed. That if Huss would submit to the Council, he would treat him with clemency; but in case he remained obstinate in his heresy, he (the Emperor) would be "the first to lead him to the wood-pile." This statement is made on the express authority of Professor Hefele, the celebrated author of the History of the Councils (Conciliengeschichte). Palacky, the famous Bohemian historian, remarks that this declaration of the Emperor immensely provoked the Bohemians, because the Emperor thus incited the Council against him; and we have the further testimony of an eye-witness, at the handing over of Huss to the secular power (Reichenthal, then canon of Constance), that the deputies of the synod prayed our lord the King and the secular court not to put Huss to death, but to spare his life and shut him up in perpetual imprisonment. As much is said by a later Zwinglian chronicler, John Stumpf. It is thus that the Catholic Church, as represented by the Council, is vindicated from the charge of having violated the safe conduct of the heretic murderer, or of having consigned him to the death which his iniquities provoked. We might add much more from the sanguinary annals of the disciples and successors of Huss, Procopius, and Zisca, but let this do for the present.

And now a few words on the inconsistencies and the self-contradictions of the lecturer, and his involuntary defense of the conduct of the Church and the Council. "Huss," he tells us, "before his appearance at Constance, had been cut off by excommunication from all intercourse with his fellow-citizens, and had gone into retirement, supported, of course, by the consciousness of his immaculate innocence and orthodoxy." And yet, in the next sentence, he lets us see him *"preaching from town to town, in the woods and in the open fields."* Again, he informs us that *"while the hereditary enemy of the Christian religion* (the Mohammedan) *was aiming to crush the Christian Church and State, Huss resisted to the utmost the preaching of the crusade, denying the right of the Church to make war for any cause."* Moreover, "*No intelligence,*" he says, "*could have been more welcome to Huss than that a council of the Universal Church would be convened at Constance;*" and no sooner is this said, than Huss is represented as refusing, when invited, to up-

pear before it. Finally, the lecturer, after deriving all his information from the enemies of the Catholic Church, one of whom is, doubtless, the infidel Professor Schenkel, of Heidelberg, leaves his hearers completely in the dark as to whether Huss was justly, or unjustly, accused of saying there "*were four persons in the Godhead, and that he, Huss, was one of them!*" Indeed, from the connection in which the statement is found, it appears that the lecturer regards it as true. For the information of our readers we here insert a connected and truthful account of Huss and the Hussites from "Bell's Wanderings of the Human Intellect:"

HUSSITES—followers of John Huss and of Jerome of Prague. They were both condemned to the stake and executed, at Constance, for their seditious opinions, in 1415. Huss, deeply tainted with the doctrines of Wickliffe, taught that the Church consisted exclusively of the just and predestinate—reprobates and sinners, according to him, making no part of this society. Hence he conclued that a bad pope, for instance, was no longer the Vicar of Jesus Christ; that bishops and priests, living in a state of sin, forfeited, of course, all claim to jurisdiction and ministerial power. This doctrine he extends even to the persons of civil magistrates and princes. "Those that are vicious and govern ill," he says, "are, *ipso facto*, stripped of all authority." Vast numbers adopted his sentiments in Bohemia and Moravia.

The consequences of such pernicious tenets are obvious: the moment any subject establishes himself judge of the conduct of his superiors, as well spiritual as temporal, and that it appears to him exceptionable, he has nothing to do but rise in arms to effect their extirpation.

Thus did this pretender to reform, under the specious plea of opposing the abuses to which the authority of the Roman Pontiffs, sometimes carried to excess, gave occasion, aim a mortal blow at the very vitals of all subordination in Church and State. He held that Christians were not obliged to obey their prelates but when their orders appeared to themselves reasonable and just; that their rule of faith was Scripture alone; with other doctrinal innovations, since adopted by the Protestants. From the censures of the Archbishop of Prague and of the Pope he appealed to the General Council of Constance; to which the King of Bohemia commanded him to give an account of his doctrine, after first obtaining for him of the Emperor Sigismund a promise of a free and safe passage through his dominions, on his way to Constance, as well as on his return from the Council, provided he should be there found orthodox, or retract his errors. Huss, on the contrary, obstinately refused to obey the Council, and continued openly to disseminate his seditious principles. For this treasonable and inflammatory conduct he was—by the civil magistrate of Constance, and not by the Council—sentenced to the flames. Neither the emperor nor the Council on this occasion did any thing inconsistent with good faith. The Council condemned his errors, and left to the emperor the part of inflicting on the criminal the punishment awarded by the law; and the emperor did no more than avenge his own cause and that of every crowned head in directing him to be legally punished when found guilty and pertinacious in his treasonable maxims. This is a right inalienable in all sovereigns, and it is an absurdity to imagine that Sigismund ever had the most distant idea of despoiling himself of it.

Mosheim, the great advocate and admirer of John Huss, himself acknowledges that the declaration which he made against the infallibility of the Catholic Church was sufficient to entitle him to the epithet of false teacher. Was, then, the Catholic Church to alter its belief, in order, with consistency, to *absolve* a person of that description? Mosheim again allows (Hist. Eccles.) that the Hussites of Bohemia *rebelled* against the Emperor Sigismund after he became their lawful sovereign, and chose to take up arms rather than submit to the decrees of the Council of Constance, pretending that Huss had been condemned unjustly. Was it then in character for an ignorant banditti, as they certainly were, to undertake to decide, as judges, what was orthodox doctrine, and what not? They did not long agree even among themselves, and soon formed two independent parties—the one denominated *Calixtins*, because they insisted upon being allowed the privilege of the chalice at Communion, requiring, moreover, that the clergy should imitate the conduct of the apostles, and that mortal sins should be punished in a manner apportioned to their enormity; the other party was called *Thaborites*, from a mountain in the vicinity of Prague, which they fortified, and to which they gave the name of *Thabor*. These were more fanatical than the former, and carried their pretensions still farther. Primitive simplicity, the abolition of the Papal authority, the absolute change of the form of worship, and the conceit of having none to preside over their society but Jesus Christ in person, who, they said, was about personally to revisit the earth, with a flambeau in one hand, and a sword in the other, in order to extirpate heresy and to purify his Church. To this class of Hussites, exclusively, Mosheim wishes to ascribe all the acts of cruelty and barbarity commited in Bohemia during the course of a bloody war which lasted sixteen years. "But," he observes, "it is difficult to decide whether the Hussites or the Catholics pushed their excesses to greater lengths." Let us suppose it, for a moment: The Hussites, at least, were the aggressors—they did not await the martyrdom of John Huss before they exercised their outrages upon the Catholics; and, though there might exist abuses in the Church, a troop of ignorant fanatics, surely, were not the fittest instruments to reform them. Mosheim admits that their maxims were *abominable*, and that from such men it was not natural to expect any thing save acts of cruelty and injustice.

In the year 1433, the fathers of the Council of Basil succeeded in reconciling the Calixtins to the Catholic Church, and indulged them in the use of the cup at the Sacred Communion. The Thaborites, on the contrary, remained incorrigible; though Mosheim tells us that, on this occasion, for the first time, they began to examine into the grounds of their religion, and to give to it a reasonable form. It was, indeed, high time they should do so, after sixteen years of blood and carnage. These reformed sectarians of John Huss now took the name of *Brethren of Bohemia*, and were also called *Picards*, or rather *Begards*: they espoused the cause of Luther when he commenced reformer, and were his precursors before they became his disciples. Hence we may account for that partiality which Protestants have always shown in favor of the Hussites. Of this so glorious an alliance Catholics do not envy them the honor. 1. It is granted by the Protestants that these their fellow-brethren in Christ were influenced—not by their zeal for religion, but by a blind and furious fanaticism, since they never thought of any plan of worship before the lapse of sixteen years, at least, after the death of their protomartyr Huss! 2. Mosheim has not condescended to inform the world in what consisted that pretended *reasonable* religion which so naturally formed a coalition with Protestantism. Indeed, that a religion, orthodox in its principles and rational in its creed, should have been the work of a frantic and infuriated rabble, is somewhat paradoxical. Luther himself had sucked in from the writings of Wickliffe and John Huss, not only his heterodox opinions, but also those sanguinary maxims which disgrace his own writings, and renewed in Germany, through the instrumentality of the Anabaptists, a part of the horrid scenes of blood and devastation, of which the Hussites had already set the example in Bohemia.

J. B. PURCELL,
Archbishop of Cincinnati.

REV. THOMAS VICKERS.

(From the *Catholic Telegraph*, January 8, 1863.)

THE undersigned, at the instance of many inquirers and friends, has resolved to publish, in book form, his letters to Rev. Thomas Vickers. This he shall do as soon as Thomas has gone through a few more of his "interesting and instructive" lectures at Hopkins' Hall. Meantime, Thomas has not ventured to give the names of the Catholics who, to his personal knowledge, are forbidden to read the Bible. He was charged with deliberate falsehood if these names were not forthcoming, and to this day, after weeks of expectancy, they are— Thomas knows why—kept in abeyance.

Again: when Archbishop Purcell quoted the Latin vulgate (Ps. xxxiii: 15), to prove that the word *persequere* had the signification of *pursue*, not *persecute*, Thomas has since somewhere defied the Archbishop to cite any classical author who gave the word in any other sense than that of *persecuting*. Well, here are quotations from the classics enough to satisfy the fastidious. The easiest mode of settling this little controversy is to open Anthon's Latin and English Dictionary at the word "persequor." The first meaning there given is, "to follow; come after; to follow or pursue eagerly or perseveringly." "Quemadmodum simus Hortensium ipsius vestigiis persccuti;" "persequi omnes vias" (Cic.) —to try all means; to seek delight in any thing; "alicujus rei oblectamenta; voluptates" (Cic.)—to follow up or practice a trade, profession, or art; "persequi artes" (Cic.)—to observe, follow, or pursue regularity, order; "persequi ordinem" (Cic.)—to adopt, to study a certain doctrine, attach one's self to a school; "academiam veterem persequamur" (Cic.)—to pursue; that is, defend one's rights by law; "a persequi bona sua lite et judicio" (Cic.)—to collect money, wills, deeds, or autographs; "persequi hereditates et syngraphas" (Cic.)— to take down a discourse in writing, short-hand or stenography; "persequi celeritate scribendi, quæ dicuntur" (Cic.)—to lead a poor life; "persequi vitam inopem" (Cic.)—to keep or accomplish commands; "mea mandata persequere"—to use diligence, smartness; "persequi sollertiam"—to survey or take a retrospect of past days; "persequere dies" (Cic.)—to explain, describe, narrate, treat of any thing; "persequi aliquid versibus, scriptura" (Cic.)—to treat of one's life; "de alicujus vita persequi."

Has Thomas blushed in pursuing this record? Is he ashamed of his falsehoods, or only rusty?

J. B. PURCELL,
Archbishop of Cincinnati.

REV. MR. VICKERS' FOURTH LECTURE,

REVIEWED BY ARCHBISHOP PURCELL.

(In the *Catholic Telegraph*, of February 26, 1868.)

The Cincinnati *Gazette*, of 3d inst., treats us to a brief analysis of the lecture at Hopkins' Hall, February 2d. Subject—Guttenberg, the inventor of printing.

A deal of extraneous, if not wholly irrelevant, matter was introduced to fill up the time, such as the rise of the Free Cities, the Hanseatic League, the overthrow of Feudalism by the merchants, the revival of Letters, and like forces—all, be it remembered, in Catholic times, all showing the prodigious activity of the Catholic mind, as testified to by these facts and the acknowledgment of such men as Emerson, Carlyle, Maitland, Hallam, and even Rev. Mr. Vickers himself, who tells us "the productions of the press increased rapidly"—but the lecturer is at special pains to hide from view the part taken by Catholic popes, bishops, priests, Benedictine monasteries and others, in multiplying, by the works they patronized or published, the "unbounded astonishment and wonder in Europe." He does not tell us that the first fruit of the joint labors of Guttenberg, Faust, and his son-in-law Schæfer, was "Durandi Rationale Divinorum officiorum," a book of Catholic prayers, in 1459.

He suppresses the truth that the press was employed

to publish the Bible in the vernacular language of Germany, *before the birth of Luther*—of which I have one or two copies in my library; he is reticent as to the number of Bibles in various languages of Europe and of Asia, Polyglotts, etc.—Ximenes' among the rest—so early given to the world by Catholic priests and Catholic enterprise. All he has to say is that "it liberated science from the power of the priesthood"—an utterance which scholars will say came with an ill grace after such splendid facts in that connection. For these shortcomings the only penance we would impose on the vapid lecturer would be the privilege, which myself and a few *ignorant* priests were allowed, last Thursday, to behold the magnificent collection of MS. and printed Bibles, Psalteries, Missals, Breviaries, Dantes, and Followings of Christ, with which our public-spirited fellow-citizen, Mr. Probasco, has endowed one of the precincts of the Queen City. There would the Rev. Mr. Vickers, if a single spark of the "Mens divinior" remain unextinguished in his bosom, fall on his knees and smite his breast in shame and sorrow for having basely traduced the Catholic Church and priesthood.

Fifth and Sixth Lectures—Subject, Savanarola. This is Mr. Vickers' orthography. It should be Savonarola.

The lecturer may first tell his story; then let the truth of history be heard.

Savonarola was born at Ferrara, on September 21st, 1452. In his youth, his favorite studies were Aristotle, Aquinas, and Plato (pretty good for a beginning in that dark age). At the age of twenty-three he entered a Dominican convent, as lay brother, in Bologna; and the lecturer tells us—no news—that it is impossible to say

how much unrequited love had to do with his choice.*
He was appointed (of course by the ignorant monks, to
deepen the ignorance of the people) lecturer in Natural
Philosophy and Metaphysics. "About" 1490 he came
(went) to Florence. There he found the prelates (how
many prelates in one city?) had no care of their flocks,
priests were given to avarice, the monks were licentious,
the women devoted to vanity, and the soldiers to vice
and crime." In Rome, at that time, the lecturer makes
him find that the vice of licentiousness prevailed, particularly among the priests, and that there were more than
the four hundred houses of ill repute recently reported
by the Cincinnati police "at this side of the Rhine," in
that city. For these and other exaggerated statements,
the lecturer leads not his hearers to the polluted and
polluting sources, other than his own mind, from which
they were derived. It is owing to the disgust of his
hearers, rather than to bad weather, that the lecturer has
been lately speaking to rather empty benches. This is
creditable to the gentlemen, but particularly to the ladies.

In his sixth lecture, he says of Savonarola: "Plebian
in his public appointments, he kindled a jealousy among
the Patricians." Now this *Plebian* must be an instance
of a new style of orthography peculiar to the lecturer;
whereas the phrase "plebian in his public appointments" baffles comprehension.

Whatever it does mean, we can not discover why it
kindled the jealousy of the Patricians. We do not see
in any of the historians we have consulted, such as
Fleury, Wetzer, and Welte, De Feller, etc., that the Pope
ever offered Savonarola a cardinal's hat, and thus gave

---

* A gratuitous inuendo of Mr. Vickers, unsupported by history.

him occasion to make use of the smart saying, that he would never wear one unless dyed in his own blood.* Pic de la Mirandole, "nephew of his uncle," might have indulged in this, or any other extravagance in his heroworship. But the haughty monk was no favorite with Alexander VI, whose excommunication he despised.

Like Sejanus, in Pagan Rome, the idol of the populace to-day may be the outlaw of their fury to-morrow. The Florentine mob idolized Savonarola at one time, they execrated him at another. He was accused of heresy by the Cordeliers, or Franciscans, and defended by his brethren, the Jacobins, or Dominicans. The proposed ordeal by fire, in which Savonarola was quite willing that one of the Dominicians should figure instead of himself, having proved a failure, Fra Hieronymo was put to the torture. During the "question" he confessed, after it he retracted, and Mr. Vickers acknowledges, notwithstanding the love of truth, for which he says he was remarkable in his youth, that he declared he would, if put on the rack, "confess and retract indefinitely." No wonder that the lecturer imitates his saint in this particular by placing to the account of the sainted De Arbues an *hundred thousand martyrs*, more or less! Finally, Savonarola, with two of his fanatical companions, was condemned to the gallows, and, after their execution, their bodies were consumed with fire and the ashes thrown into the Arno. After this account of Brother Jerome by Rev. Mr. Vickers, with my own running commentary, I now present the following highly interesting and authentic sketch of his career, related by Darras in his

---

*The offer of a cardinal's hat rests on the authority of his admirer, the Dominican author of the "Hommes Illustres," &c., who says a Dominican bishop told the Dominican legate to ask this favor from the Pope for Savonarola.

Ecclesiastical History. With this and other Catholic historians, I deplore the pride that impelled Savonarola to his ruin; and I regard his fate as a warning to all who indulge to excess in their denunciation of the vices of their fellow-men, whether historical or cotemporary, and who are inconsistent enough to violate the laws which they had themselves established and sworn to obey.

1st N. B. Will Rev. Mr. Vickers confess his inexcusable ignorance in quoting Tertullian against the Roman supremacy in a book, "*De præscriptione hæreticorum*"? whereas he never wrote a book with such a title. This is an absurd and palpable blunder of the lecturer.

2d N. B. Will the reader and the Rev. Paul Mohr, *Bantam*, of Clermont County, the indorser of Mr. Vickers, look to the latter's book (pp. 38, 81) where he makes the tardy confession of his having attributed to Aquinas, as reproached by Archbishop Purcell, words which are not to be found in Aquinas. "Oh," says Mr. Vickers, "*I did not pretend to give the exact words.*"

J. B. PURCELL,
Archbishop of Cincinnati.

21. Florence had, meanwhile, been made the scene of events, perhaps without example in human annals. They have conferred its celebrity upon the name of Jerome Savonarola. Jerome was a Dominican monk and prior of the Convent of St. Mark. He seemed to have been destined for the retreat of the cloister, where his austerity and fervor were the edification of his religious brethren. But Fra Girolamo had received the dangerous endowment of genius, and his virtue was, unhappily, too weak to bear the splendid gift. Savonarola was un-

known; he was placed in the pulpit, and his eloquence won him a power which met and overcame that of the princely Medici. When Charles VIII had entered Florence, he demanded from the citizens one hundred and twenty thousand gold crowns, which he needed to continue his campaign. Twenty-four hours were allowed to collect the sum. The required amount could not be raised, and the irritated monarch threatened to destroy the city. The terrified inhabitants hastened to the cell of the Dominican monk. "I will go to the king," said Jerome, who had repeatedly warned the people, for more than a year past, that God was about to punish their crimes by giving them up to the power of the French. Savonarola appeared at the palace gates, but was refused admittance; he persevered in his efforts, and was at length led before the king. Drawing a crucifix from beneath his religious habit and holding it up before Charles, he exclaimed, "Prince, do you know this sign? It is the image of Christ, who died on the cross for you, and for me, and for all of us, and who, with his last breath, implored pardon for his murderers. If you will not hear me, you will at least hear him who speaks by my mouth, the King of kings, who gives victory to faithful princes, who casts down the wicked. Unless you renounce your cruel design of destroying this wretched city, the tears of so many guiltless victims will plead to heaven with a power far different from that of your armies and your cannon. What are numbers and strength before the Lord? Moses and Joshua triumphed over their enemies by prayer; we, too, will use the arms of prayer, if you will not relent. Prince, will you be merciful?" The monk, as he spoke, held up before the king the image of the Crucified Redeemer. Charles was overcome, and abandoned his fatal project. His impassioned eloquence was always a most powerful weapon in the hands of the religious, and Savonarola soon found another occasion to try its efficacy. The Medici were driven from Florence by a popular revolution; a new form of government was to be established, and the Dominican prior was called upon to frame it. Retiring for a few days from the pulpit, he set himself to his new task and drew up a constitution on the plan of the Venetian. It was read by him, in the cathedral, before the magistrates and the people; and, from that moment, the monk was at once priest, magistrate, judge, and lawgiver. He used his boundless influence only for the greater glory of God, with results which, at the present day, may seem incredible. By his order, eight pyramids were erected in the public square, and upon them were promiscuously piled dangerous books, indecent ornaments, dice, cards, and other instruments of vice; the whole was then given to the flames. All the citizens were present at this holocaust of the sensual world, offered up to the God of penance and mortification.

22. So far Savonarola had shown himself worthy of his high renown; but the Spirit of God, which animated the first period of his life, seemed to have withdrawn its guidance from the second. An instant sufficed to dispel, like a light cloud, all the prestige which had attended his name. The constitution given by him to the Florentines decreed, among other articles, that every citizen condemned for a political fault should have the right to appeal to the great council of the nation. Five conspirators, who had been arrested and con-

demned to capital punishment, availed themselves of
the new law and appealed to the grand council. Savonarola opposed the appeal, and they were executed.
The general indignation broke out into a fearful storm.
The religious replied only by invectives hurled from
the pulpit, not only against vices, but against individuals. The Roman court, the Pope, and the cardinals
were all included in his sweeping denunciations. The
secular clergy withdrew their support, the people gave
free rein to their fury, and a thousand arms were raised
to tear down the idol of yesterday. From all sides arose
a demand for prompt and just satisfaction. The judgment of the important case was left to Alexander VI.
The Pope enjoined silence in the matter until sentence
should have been pronounced upon the culprit, who
was, at the same time, requested to appear in Rome
to explain and justify his conduct. Savonarola refused, and continued his furious harangues. A second
and a third admonition, likewise unheeded, were followed
by a sentence of excommunication, publicly read in all
the churches in Florence. The proud reformer had rejected the advances of mercy, laughed at the thunders
of the Church, persisted in his sacrilegious preaching,
and now stood in open revolt against the supreme head
of the Christian world. The schismatic was tried before the tribunal of the Archbishop of Florence; Savonarola suffered death, after having made his confession and received the body of the Savior, with the
plenary indulgence, *in articulo mortis*, sent by the Pope,
A. D. 1498. Thus perished one of the most splendid
intellects of the fifteenth century—a victim of his own
ungovernable pride.

REVIEW.

Having concluded all that I thought it necessary to write in answer to the charges brought against the Catholic Church—her claims, her teachings, and her spirit—by Rev. Mr. Vickers, I had resolved to add no more, until I had seen two addresses in which the gentleman uncoiled himself, on the 26th of April and 10th of May, in Indianapolis and Cincinnati, to the full extent of his serpentine proportions. From these effusions, as I find them in the Indianapolis *Sentinel* and the Cincinnati *Daily Times,* I propose to make a few extracts, that the Christian reader may see the condition of an infidelized mind. The autopsy will furnish the best refutation of the reviler's theories, his vain assumptions, and his arrogant denunciations of ecclesiasticism and the Bible.

In his sermon of the 26th of April, the preacher, who, like a man traveling on a rail car, thinks the whole world is moving in his direction, tells us that the "old creeds are breaking up;" and that "what has hitherto been regarded as essential to ecclesiastical life is rapidly losing, or has already lost, its hold on the minds of the people." We have no doubt that Mr. V. indulges in this illusion. The wish is father to the thought, and the only proof that facts will warrant for the rash assertion. Now, in the name of all that is just, and truthful, and rational, we ask him where in Cincinnati, where the progress of the Catholic faith has been, and is, so marvelous; where in Boston, New York, Philadelphia, Pittsburg, Baltimore, St. Louis, Chicago, New Orleans, Mobile, Milwaukee, is the evidence that the Catholic faith is retrograding in the number of its worshipers, its churches, its institutions of learning, its hospitals, asylums, orphanages? Where in the old world—in Ireland, England, France, Germany, or New Australia—do we discover the "decay of faith;" "faith in a state of eclipse;" the "suspense of faith," which Mr. V., through Protestant spectacles, sees all around, and from which he tells us Protestantism, "though shut up to the use of fraud in one or the other of its Protean forms," does not hesitate to use all the resources in its power to rescue? The Catholic Church has no need to resort to such expedients; the evil designated exists not in her borders. She steadily continues, not only in undiminished, but in constantly-increasing numbers, conquering and to conquer, on her road to heaven. He that sees this not is blind; he that asserts the contrary does not speak the truth.

Again, the Ishmaelite tells us that ecclesiasticism, whether it be "Jewish, Roman Catholic, Protestant, or only Unitarian, is always intolerant. It annihilated (and here *it* is, in Mr. Vickers' sense, but another name for God) the Canaanites, it crucified Jesus, it stoned Stephen to death, it founded the inquisition, it burned Servetus, it drove the Puritans out of England, it hanged Mary Dyer on Boston Commons, it prayed God to put a hook into the jaws of Theodore Parker while living, and after his death it declared,-from an Unitarian pulpit (as if in the very delirium of intolerance and meanness), that he did not accept the conditions of salvation."

In the same strain he says (falsely, at least, as far as the Catholic Church is concerned) that "belief, or mere intellectual assent, without piety or morality, is made to take the place of life; so that he who believes in the dogmas of the Church, the total depravity of human nature, a personal devil, and an eternal hell, the incarnation of God in the person of Jesus of Nazareth, and the atonement through his death on the cross, and other such absurdities, has complied with the essential conditions of salvation." That intellectual assent was not made by the Church the all-sufficient condition of salvation, we have Mr. Vickers' acknowledgment; for he tells us in the opening sentence of his sermon of the 10th of May, forgetting or contradicting what he had said on the 26th of April, that the Church had "peterized Paul and paulinized Peter. The cry of Peter *or* Paul, works or faith, had changed to the watchword of Peter *and* Paul, works and faith." After this unblushing falsehood, it will excite no surprise that he proceeds to the indecency of saying that the free Spirit is dispensed through an ecclesiastical bellows, and that it is said no man can live unless he keep the nozzle "in his mouth." This reminds me of the vulgarity of the Voltairian wit regarding the prophet's breakfast, so effectually retorted on the cynic in the Jewish Letters by the Abbé Guenee, and the infidel Taylor's suggestion, in England, fifty years ago, that "they were the swine into which the devils entered, and not the Lamb, that took away the sins of the world." It almost provokes me to say that Mr. Vickers' self-abasing *followers* derive their inspiration from him.

"Ou le dos
Perd ser nom."

In his sermon of the 10th of May, he makes Christ, and Peter (who he says *never was in Rome*, whereas our old convert-friend, Judge Mitchel, after a thorough study of history, truly says the "Chair of Peter is as clear in Rome as the throne of the Cæsars"), and Clement, Linus, and Anacletus all fictitious persons; that the power given to the apostles to "bind and loose," as recorded in the Gospels, was *put into his mouth* by the evangelists, but never uttered; that "the belief in God and the devil are both creations of fancy." And yet (who could believe if he were not himself the witness?) Mr. Vickers is constrained, in the same sermon, to neutralize much of his injustice to the Catholic Church by confessing that she has fulfilled a great mission: "She carried the Christian view of life and Christian civilization to nations who could get hold of the spiritual essence of Christianity only through imagination and faith; she proclaimed the equality of all men before God; and whatever miracles she did not work, she performed the greatest miracles of self-sacrificing love and mercy. She brought about a great unity of man in faith; she attempted, in a rude way, to put the fundamental thought of Christianity into life: that the Spirit is supreme, and the eternal more than the temporal. It was this thought that gave rise to the profound consciousness of sin, upon which her whole scheme of life is based. Man's chief, only care, is to save his soul. The Church contained an infinity, a miraculous world of love, and an ineffable treasury of spiritual life." Here the devil again lays hold on Mr. Vickers, and I refuse to copy the words that follow in in the sermon.

I have some hope that Mr. Vickers, who is still a

young man, will discover the error of his ways and forget the antichristian lessons which the infidel professors of Heidelberg have taught him. With all his anti-ecclesiastical, anti-social theorizing, I think I still discover traces of a higher nature and a better spirit, originally given him by God, and for a nobler purpose than that to which his life and intellect are now misapplied. To help him to this emancipation from the fetters that bind him to a false mission, we devote the remainder of the space which the "signature," as the printers call it, allows us, to the beautiful and truthful testimony to the Catholic Church by Mr. Dix, a non-Catholic, of Massachusetts, and commend it, at parting, to Rev. Mr. Vickers and all who seek the saving truth.

J. B. PURCELL,

Archbishop of Cincinnati.

"Beauty and order being the same thing, and religious truth being the beauty of holiness, Christ, who was truth in person, must have made his Church the friend and upholder of all beauty and order; and so it has proved for eighteen hundred years. The Church has been the celestial crucible in which whatever of human art or invention had within it the essential attributes of higher and spiritual goodness has been purified and adapted to the service of religion. Has poetry sought to please the imaginations of men? the Church of Christ unfolded before her the annals of Christianity, with her grand central sacrifice of infinite love, and all her demonstrations of heroic suffering and courageous faith; and poetry drew holier inspiration from the view, and incited men, by higher motives, to a higher life. Have painting and sculpture sought to represent objects of refining grace and sublimity? the Church of Christ persuaded them to look into the records of the Christian past, and there they found treasures of beauty and splendor, devotion and martyrdom, whose wealth of illustration as examples, incentives, and memorials, art has not exhausted for centuries, and will never exhaust. Christian history is the inexhaustible quarry of whatever is most noble and heroic in man, purified by the grace of God. Has architecture sought to invest stone with the attributes of spiritual and intellectual grace? the Church of God has so portrayed before her the sublimities of the Christian faith that she knelt at her feet in veneration, and thenceforth consecrated herself to build enduring structures, which, the more they show of human power and skill, the more they persuade men to the worship of God. Has eloquence sought to nerve men for the grand conflicts of life? the Church of Christ has touched the lips of eloquence with living fire from her altar, until have sprung forth words that flamed with love to man and love to God. Has music sought to weave her entrancing spells around the heart and soul? the Church of Christ has breathed into music her own divine being, until the music of the Church seems like beatific worship, and worship on earth like beatific music.

"As in these respects, so in others, the Church has made a holy conquest of whatever is noblest among the endowments of men. In speaking of Catholic history, even from the secular point of view, it may be justly said that nowhere else has there been such wonderful discernment of the various capacities of the human mind, and of their various adaptations. Tenacious of the truth and of all its prerogatives, the Catholic Church has, nevertheless, allowed a wide liberty of thought. That the Catholic Church has narrowed the understandings of men, is a singular charge to make in the face of the schools of Catholic philosophy, in which men of varying mental structure, training, or habits of thought, have had full, free play of their faculties. And where else have there been so many free and varying activities as in the Catholic Church? The false charge that the Church fetters the minds and movements of men may be traced to the fact that all Catholic diversities of thought have converged, like different rays of light, in the elucidation of truth; and that varying modes of Catholic action have had one object—the advancement of truth.

"Here is the intended force of all these illustrations, for they have had a logical purpose. The world will never outgrow the Church. All the boasted improvements in science, in art, in civilization, so far from impeding the Church of Christ, and making her existence no longer needed, will, at the same time, advance her power, and make her more needed than ever. If in the middle ages, when society was in the process of transition from the old to the new, the Church was preëminently needed to keep what was just and right and true in the older forms of civilization, and gradually to adapt to them what was just and right and true in the newer developments of society, most truly is the Church needed now, when there exists a perfect chaos of opinions, and when a part of the civilized world is in another transition, from the aimless, rudderless vagaries of Protestantism to the solid rock of Catholicity. If ever the voice of authority was needed, like the voice of the angel of God, heard amid and above the howlings of the storm, it is needed now.

"Much false reasoning has been uttered about the 'unchangeable Church,' as though, because 'unchangeable,' it was not adapted to a changing and striving world, when, in truth, for the very reason that the Church of Christ is unchangeably true, she is required and adapted for all the changes and emergencies of time. Who ever heard a sailor complain of the mariner's compass, because, on account of its unchangeable obstinacy, it would not conform to his private judgments and caprices about the right course? No one. It is for the very reason that the mariner's compass is unchangeably true to the eternal law of magnetic attraction, under all circumstances, and in all places, that it is the unerring guide among the whirlwinds and heavings of the great deep. Catholicity is the mariner's compass upon a greater deep—even that of the wild and rolling, beating ocean of humanity, pointing, amid sunny calms, or gentle winds, or raging gales, unerringly to the cross of Jesus Christ, as the needle of the mariner's compass points to the north—guiding, age after age, her precious freight of immortal souls to the harbor of infinite and unending joy.

"The force of this illustration is all the stronger that the mariner's compass is a human adaptation of an immutable law of nature to navigation, while the Church of the living God is divine alike in origin and application, and has existed from the beginning, unchangeable, like God himself, yet adapting herself to the wants of every age. The Church of God is like his own infinite providence, in which unchangeable truth meets in the harmony of mercy the innumerable changes of human need.

"Much has been written, and more said, about 'the church of the future,' as though it were to be some millennial manifestation altogether different from the historic church; but the church of the future which is not also the church of the past and of the present can be no church; for a true church must reach to the ages back as to those before. If the continuity is broken, truth is broken, and can not be restored. As for eighteen centuries there have been no forms of civil society, no calms or tempests in the moral, political, social, or religious world, in which the Catholic Church has not been true to the organic principles of her divine life, even the enemy of Catholicity should admit—that fact being granted—that the presumption is on her side that she will be equally true to those principles during the centuries that are to come. He may deny that the Church has been true, and, consequently, that she will be true, but he will not admit one proposition and deny the other; he will admit both, or deny both; in other words, he will admit, equally with the friend of Catholicity, the identity of the Church, past, present, and to come. Now, it will be impossible for a friend or enemy of the Catholic Church, from her beginning to this very day, to point to an hour when she was not a living Church. It is, then, probable that she will continue to be a living Church. But where, since the promulgation of Christianity to this time, has existed a body of Christian believers which, for the quality of continual existence, has so good a right to be called the Church of Christ as the Catholic Church? Considering her numbers, extent, and duration, that church has been preeminently the church of the past; considering numbers, extent, and duration, that church is preëminently the church of the present; considering all analogies and probabilities, then the Catholic Church will be preëminently the church of the future.

"In truth, the vindictive anger of the enemies of the Catholic Church, in whatever form of opposition it may be shown, proceeds from the fact, not that she is the dead church of the past, as she is sometimes called, for there would be no reason to war with the dead, but because she is, as she has been and will be, the living church. The Catholic Church is hated, not for being too dead, but for being too living. She has seen the birth and death of countless 'improvements' of her principles, and has received with gladness into her fold many an eager and conscientious inquirer for the 'new church,' who has at length reached an end of his wanderings and a solution of his doubts in finding, with tears of rapturous submission, that the new church, for which he was seeking, is the same church which has stood for ages—ever old, yet ever new, because representing Him who is alike the living God and the Ancient of Days.

"The Catholic Church, so frequently and unjustly denounced as ever behind the age, or even as facing the past, has been foremost in all parts of the world. She has sent her faithful soldiers of the cross where the spirit of commerce dared not go; she was the first in the east and the first in the west. It was her lamp of divine light which dispelled the gloomy terrors of the barbarous north of Europe; it was her scepter of celestial beauty which, under the guidance of heaven, transformed the political and social wreck of southern Europe into order. In what part of the world which man could reach has she not planted the cross? Where on the face of the earth is the mountain whose craggy sides have not, at one time or another, sent back into the sounding air the echoes of Catholic worship?

"Daniel Webster gave a vivid picture of the extent of the power of England in what I think to be the grandest sentence which America has contributed to the common treasure of English literature. He said:

"'The morning drum beat, following the sun, and keeping company with the hours, circles the earth daily with one unbroken strain of the martial airs of England.'

"That grand figure of speech may be applied to the extent of the Catholic Church. Yet it is not by martial airs, but by hymns of praise, and penitential orisons, and the continuous sacrifice that the Catholic Church daily celebrates, 'from the rising of the sun unto the going down of the same,' the triumphant march of the Prince of Peace. How like 'the sound of many waters' roll hourly heavenward the anthems of Catholic worship throughout the world! Not only is every moment of every day consecrated by Catholic hymns sung somewhere on earth, but how majestically roll down through eighteen hundred years the unbroken anthems of Catholic devotion! Minute after minute, hour after hour, day after day, night after night, month after month, year after year, century after century, the holy strains go on unending. To the mind's ear seem blended in one almost overpowering flood of holy harmony the unnumbered voices which have sounded from the very hour when the shepherds of Bethlehem heard the angelic songs to this very moment, when, somewhere, Catholic voices are chanting praise to the Lord and Savior of men."

THE CHEAPEST SONG BOOK.

SCHOOL RECREATIONS:

Or, The Catholic Teacher's Companion. Containing 79 Hymns and 51 Songs, compiled for the use of Catholic Schools, with the approbation of the Most Rev. J. B. PURCELL, Archbishop of Cincinnati; Rt. Rev. G. A. CARRELL, Bishop of Covington; and Rt. Rev. S. H. ROSECRANS, Bishop of Columbus, O.

8vo, 94 pages. Price, 35 cents.

We refer to the remarks made by the Catholic Press.

THE CATHOLIC TELEGRAPH, OF CINCINNATI.

"This work fills a want long felt; a book intended solely for the school-room, combining piety with innocent amusement. With a few exceptions, the hymns are old and well known to our Catholic youth, and have been selected as well with a view to their simplicity and popularity as for their fitness for children's voices. The songs are amusing as well as instructive, and will help to relieve the dull tedium of school hours. We cordially and earnestly recommend its use in our Catholic schools."

THE CATHOLIC, OF PITTSBURG.

"This is a collection of approved Hymns and popular Songs, set to music. It will be found of great use in the school-room, and we think our teachers would do well to introduce among their children a taste for that study to which this little book is devoted. Our children, when at school, could be taught most of the hymns used in the offices of the Church. They might also be taught to chant vespers, and sing some of the simpler masses used in our choirs. Then why is it not done? Would not the acquisition of such a degree of vocal music be of use to the children, and a great benefit to priest and people? and might not our schools be made to serve as feeders to our choirs, which many pastors find it so difficult to organize and maintain?"

THE CATHOLIC MIRROR, OF BALTIMORE.

"Our hasty inspection of this little school-book impressed us most favorably. It consists of a compilation of Catholic Hymns and the Vespers, all arranged with appropriate music. Beside these, there are a number of popular melodies appended to the book. It can not fail to interest and captivate the young, and make for them a wholesome school exercise."

THE PILOT, OF BOSTON.

"This little work contains a selection of Hymns and Songs for the use of our schools—week and Sunday-schools—and it is published with the approbation of the Most Rev. J. B. Purcell, Archbishop of Cincinnati. The pieces have been selected for the purpose of relieving the tedium of long school hours. The idea is good, and we hope our teachers of parochial and Sunday-schools will follow it."

www.ingramcontent.com/pod-product-compliance
Lightning Source LLC
Chambersburg PA
CBHW020911230426
43666CB00008B/1413